THE RANTS

**DENNIS
MILLER**

THE
RANTS

DOUBLEDAY new york london toronto sydney auckland

PUBLISHED BY DOUBLEDAY a division of
Bantam Doubleday Dell Publishing Group, Inc.
1540 Broadway, New York, New York 10036

DOUBLEDAY and the portrayal of an anchor with a dolphin
are trademarks of Doubleday, a division of
Bantam Doubleday Dell Publishing Group, Inc.

BOOK DESIGN BY TERRY KARYDES

ISBN 0-385-47804-6

FOR ALI, HOLDEN, AND MARLON
You are the loves of my life

contents

preface

I HOPE YOU FIND WHAT FOLLOWS TO BE AN
amusing trifle. These rants are sometimes lacerated
for being flimsy. I'm fine with that. I don't want to
change your mind. I just want to make you laugh.
I've dated some of these because they refer to a
specific issue at a specific time. Many rants were
performed for my HBO show "Dennis Miller Live"
over the last three seasons. I'd like to thank Jeff
Cesario, Eddie Feldman, Greg Greenberg, David

Feldman, Ed Driscoll, Kevin Rooney, Bill Braudis, Leah Krinsky, and Rick Overton for their assistance on these rants.

I'd also like to thank David Gernert at Doubleday, Kevin Slattery, and Marc Gurvitz. Also Jeff Bewkes, Chris Albrecht, and Carolyn Strauss at HBO. And, most important, I'd like to thank Michael Fuchs for his unwavering belief in me.

Now I don't want to get off on a rant here, but . . .

THE RANTS

liberals—

a

dying

breed?

A RECENT SURVEY SHOWED THAT IN LAST
November's election, only 18 percent of voters
identified themselves as liberals. Wow. Liberals are
running for cover faster than Mark Fuhrman at the
Apollo Theater.

Now I don't want to get off on a rant here, but
along with the KGB and Steve Nicks, liberals
seem to belong nowadays under the "Jeopardy!"

heading: "Things Which No Longer Have Any Fucking Relevance Whatsoever." I know for me, liberalism died when the Archies broke up.

It really died though when all the middle-class kids who had been in the protest movement because Mommy and Daddy were footing the bill for their pot and Buffy Sainte-Marie albums found themselves in the big, cruel world with spouses and families to support. And nothing makes being a tool of the military-industrial complex look better than a nice, fat paycheck at the end of every week. If I had a hammer, I'd hammer out danger all over this land, but I got house payments to make, okay, Arlo?

Oh, you can still spot occasional dyed-in-the-wool liberals in their threadbare "Mondale '84" T-shirts having a decaf latte and a nonfat three-berry chocolate chip scone at a Barnes & Noble coffee bar, reading Joan Didion. That is if they can even get out of the house. Hell, it's nearly impossible for today's liberals to dress themselves trying to keep straight which color ribbon goes with what cause.

Bill Clinton has been trying to shake off his liberal label like it was a ski parka in an overheated station wagon.

You know there used to be two parties—Democrat and Republican, and, *separate from that,* two schools of political thought—liberal and conservative. Anybody remember liberal Republicans like Nelson Rockefeller and George

Romney? Today, a liberal Republican is one who thinks a condemned man getting death by injection should be laid out on a comfy mattress.

The word "liberal" has replaced "Communist" as the red flag neo-conservatives wave in your face to denote what's wrong in this country. People are even making *me* out a liberal, when in actuality I'm a pragmatist, which means I think everybody is an asshole but me.

With the threat of communism gone, the power elite no longer has to be on their best behavior. And right now, you have as good a chance of seeing tolerance from them as you do Newt Gingrich dirty dancing with Harvey Fierstein.

Since the '92 elections, the Republicans are so power-hungry they're careening through our hallowed legislative halls like Gary Busey trying to find the john at House of Blues.

What's even more pathetic is the Democratic response. They can't even agree on which shade of white to use for the surrender flag. Some quit, others are now teaching a course in Defeatist Studies at Emerson, and those few that stayed in politics, hey, they dove to their right quicker than Brooks Robinson. Today's liberal leaders bring so much baggage with them they need a skycap— Jesse Jackson, Ted Kennedy, Gary Hart.

You don't think liberals can be tough? I've got three words and one initial for you—Richard J. Daley, Senior. The late don, excuse me, mayor of Chicago. Daley made Newt Gingrich look like a head shop clerk in Haight-Ashbury. Then there was Hubert Humphrey, Lyndon Johnson, or even Illinois Senator Everett Dirksen, who could've lowered his bifocals and made Bob Packwood resign just by staring at that fuckin' lowlife till he ran out of the Senate chambers.

What the hell happened to liberals? Well, they've been feeling the pulse of the American public about as accurately as the Pepsi Clear execs. Too many liberals settled into power like a fat guy in a hammock after a double deep-dish, extra-cheese-inside-the-crust, extra-cheese-inside-that-cheese, five-meat Sasquatch pizza followed by a Baskin-Robbins Mega-Gutbuster Tin Roof-Parfait-Accompli Sundae. When it came to spending bucks, liberals were the original *Waterworld* producers. When it came to big government, they got rubber stamp bursitis. And when it came to special interest groups, they drew up the schematics that now allow PACs to control three fifths of the fucking galaxy.

But as bloated as liberal politics has become, it grew from lean and noble roots—the battle of the working class against the ruling class, the fight for the poor, the struggle of the underdog immigrant—literally, the battle for human rights, right here in this country. We can't afford to forget that.

Remember Mario Cuomo's speech at the '84 Democratic Convention? It was a stunning bolt of lightning that, if only for a brief moment, galvanized the American spirit in the hearts and minds of its people. It was electrifying prose fueled by brains, guts, and compassion, and it made you proud to be an American. Now compare that to the only memorable Republican speech of the last decade— Pat Buchanan's derisive, petty, hate-filled diatribe at the '92 GOP Convention There may not be a member of the current crop of American conservatives who could match Cuomo's speech. I think they may lack the compassion. Their conscience doesn't seem to bother them enough.

So, as far as the nuts-and-bolts legislative details are concerned, liberalism is most probably dead, and it doesn't look like a whole lot of us are gonna be at that wake. But when it comes to the ongoing battle over reshaping this ethereal thing we've dubbed the American spirit, well, liberalism had better be very much alive and breathing fire, or we have truly lost our way as a nation.

Of course, that's just my opinion. I could be wrong.

the

religious

right

NOW I DON'T WANT TO GET OFF ON A RANT HERE,
but don't these radical religious right leaders scare
you a little? I'm not talking about good simple religious folk here. I empathize with you people. I
know you're frightened. It looks like the bad guys
are winning. And I know you want to do the good
Christian thing and save some of the bad guys, but
you're probably preaching to the unconvertible.
This is a long trail ride, and occasionally a satanic

heifer or two is gonna head over the ridge and go off on their own. Let them go. Quit trying to set God up on blind dates with people he has nothing in common with. Well, anyway, you're good people and I got no quarrel with you, Atticus. I'm talking about the overzealous ones. The ones with that bloodless, glazed-over "Prophets of the Caribbean" look. You know, the ones who look like the guys who kept Howard Hughes alive those last three years. Let's run down our roster of modern-day Pharisees:

Jerry Falwell, with his big hillbilly grin concealing his hatred for you and the fun you can have with your nasty little genitals.

Then we've got Pat Robertson, the Dixie charlatan who contends he held counsel with God, saw Jesus, and has it on good authority from the Holy Ghost that "Cuber" has an arsenal of nuke-you-ler weapons aimed at the United States.

And our good friend Ollie North, who quivers with religious fervor while conveniently forgetting he was a belligerent liar who abused the authority of his position. You know I have no doubt that God will forgive Lieutenant Colonel North one day. I just don't think our courts should have.

These modern-day Torquemadas can't wait to seize the reins and begin slaughtering the nonbelievers. And if you don't think they'll do it—if you don't think you'll be on the short list for a public roasting à la Joan of Arc, well, you better stop dancing around the pagan Maypole and think again, Caligula.

Now I am sure to many of those in the Radical Right, I probably appear to be a bitter, cranky pragmatist with the mouth of a stevedore, and the soul of a heretic. But I do, believe it or not, consider myself to be a Christian—and I'm sorry, you just don't go shooting doctors. If a judgment's to be made, God gets to make it. Not you. Him. You are Barney Fife. Keep your bullet in your shirt pocket. All right?

You know, God is Andy Taylor. If abortion is wrong, and I believe in many instances it is, somewhere down the line God's gonna let you know about it. And believe me, God paybacks are an eternal bitch. Somebody else's abortion is none of your business. And listen, if you really believe that your God is telling you to kill an abortionist in his name, then you've got to crush some tinfoil on your antenna, pal, because you're gettin' some heavy interference.

And you know, while I'm at it, I don't care what arcane passage you pull out of the Old Testament and run through your Jeremiah-begat-Jedediah Decoder Ring, one of the definitive tenets of Christianity is tolerance. Trust me, there's no version of the Bible that says Love thy neighbor unless he's a Peter Allen fan. Any supposedly Christian doctrine must have at the core a belief in the concept of unqualified love for your fellow man. Unless of course he proves himself to be a total asshole. Then you can ditch him. Sure, God understands that, who do you think booked Satan's flight? What he can't understand is turning against someone because you don't happen to agree with their sexual preference. Forget your linear, biblical interpretation that tells you to ostracize gays, and follow your heart. It's like when your driving test instructor would tell you to run the stop sign. And you would, and then he'd flunk you. And you'd say, "But you told me to." And he'd say, "Sorry, but you never run a stop sign." And you never carpet bomb a group of people with hate because they're different from you. Case closed, Tailgunner Joe.

And tolerance should extend to ideas as well. A schoolbook cannot corrupt your child, especially one whose main characters are a Scarecrow, a Tin Man, and a Cowardly Lion. And if you truly think your kid's character depends on prayer, then damn it, pray with your kid—at home! Stop fobbing off on the public school system your responsibilities as a parent. The schools are there to teach your kids to read, write, and add—skills they will need if they are going to apply for and wisely invest their unemployment checks one day.

And if you're sold on prayer as a diving board into the day, get up a few minutes early, forgo the trip to the 7-Eleven for a jeroboam of Colombian blend, sit down with your kids you profess to love so much, and lead them in prayer.

Look, I realize this is America—everybody has the right to organize. The Democratic Party should try it sometime. But you know something, the members of the Radical Religious Right have to get it through their skulls: Separation of Church and State. Separate. Not together. Apart. Like Burt and Loni. One here and one there. The founding fathers set it up like that because back home in merry old England they witnessed scenes of theocratic horror that would have made even Quentin Tarantino puke.

I can only hope the Radical Right's grab for political power will eventually prove to be their Holy Waterloo.

I know we don't like to vote—marking your ballot nowadays is like choosing between the 3 A.M. showing of *Beastmaster* on Showtime and the 3 A.M. showing of *Beastmaster* 2 on Cinemax.

But the less we involve ourselves in the political process, the more special interest groups and fanatics move in.

So vote, and remember this when you're alone in the booth with just you and your lever: The Radical Right believes the word "Right" does not simply denote their placement on the political spectrum, but also their sanctimoniously smug assertion that "right" is exactly what they are on any and all issues. Amen.

Of course, that's just my opinion. I could be wrong.

our

legal

system

NOW I DON'T WANT TO GET OFF ON A RANT HERE, but you know the drill. You're walking home from the Frogurt shop one night, you're stopped by a young drifter who wants directions—and a smoke, if you have one. You don't. You're sorry, but you don't smoke. Okay, he says. And as you walk away, he shoots you in the back of the head, your half-eaten, razzleberry Frogurt and your left eye spattering a young woman twenty yards across the street.

Shortly thereafter, the police happen to pick up the young man for jaywalking, and find him with the still-warm gun in his pocket and your still-cold cone in his hand. He is then identified by the woman and arraigned.

But then, as you watch—perched on a hot poker in the eighth concentric circle of Dante's E-Z Bake—the legal system starts to kill you all over again.

The gun isn't admissible as evidence because it was found without probable cause. After all, they had only stopped him for jaywalking at that point. And the woman is discredited as an eyewitness because she usually wears glasses, and that dusky night she wasn't wearing them, the truth being, she just needs them for reading. Besides, the defense attorney reveals, she lives in a neighborhood with a porn theater, and what does that make her?

Plus, this fellow who shot you—his attorney will tell you he was once squat-humped by a Good Humor man, and you were taunting him with your razzleberry Frogurt delight.

Now, and as you stand there next to Yossarian in the great beyond and watch this cruel and ironic Catch-22 unfold—this insane sequence of events that leads up to the dismissal of all charges against the man who ended your life on that fine summer evening—as you watch this bizarre, almost synaptic set of occurrences fall into place like a chain of perverse dominoes that has been kicked over by Rube Goldberg—all you can think to yourself is, "Hey, I know where I've seen this before! *Mouse Trap!*"

And if you think I was stretchin' it with that little parable, well just look at the newspaper, folks. On Tuesday of this week, two hundred forty pounds of cocaine was disallowed as evidence in a drug case because the trooper who found it stopped the suspects' car for failure to display a front license plate. The case was thrown out because, legally, Pennsylvania only requires a rear plate.

Well you know something? That's just exquisite bullshit. And I know. And I know that every ACLU hysteric in the country is now jumping up in bed screaming, "Rules of evidence! Rules of evidence!"

But I think I speak for the general public, guys, when I say, "Take your nit-picking, neurotic little rules of evidence and stick 'em up your understanding ass," because, quite frankly, I haven't seen judgment this bad since I lost to Sinbad on "Star Search." Yeah, yeah, not that I dwell on that.

The frightening reality is every day this society seems to make its legal decisions in much the same way the Archies picked their vacation spots—blindfold Jughead, give him a dart, and spin the globe.

And what do most of these mindless decisions have in common? Well, twelve things—the jury.

The entire American legal system is based on the premise of trial by jury and the only way you can get on a jury is if you prove beyond a shadow of a doubt that you don't know shit about the case you are about to try. And you know something, after we've picked them, we then load juries down with such a yoke of admonition, stipulation, and cautionary notes from the judge that they begin to suffer from the jurisprudence equivalent of sexual performance anxiety. Nobody can go into the jury room anymore and achieve a good solid Code of Hammurabi hard-on because good old-fashioned common sense and a primal notion of right and wrong have been supplanted by lawyers' tricks and haberdashery.

Why should it matter in the least how the Menendez brothers *looked* in the courtroom? The simple fact that you can sport a nice cable-knit sweater, and trim the hair on the back of your neck to Pythagorean precision, and actually have that help you in the courtroom after you've dusted your mother with a shotgun is an insult to the intelligence of the living and a sacrilege against the memory of the dead.

And you know something, nice clothes are just the beginning. We've got all sorts of reasons to let criminals walk: Imperfect self-defense, temporary insanity, low blood sugar insanity . . .

"Oh, I see, you wouldn't have killed that family if you'd had a Zag Nut bar. Right? Yeah. Dick, Perry, put the mattress away, I found some mini Butterfingers in the fridge."

Watching the trust we had in the legal system disappear has been a sad, confusing experience, like watching smoke from a book-burning taint a cloudless sky. In the past, we revered the legal system as the backbone of democracy. Now we quite frankly fear it—its linguistic fog, the casualness of the brutal transactions, the sheer density of its unconcern. Somebody has their thumb on the scales of justice, folks. "And he's out of order, I'm out of order, the whole fucking system is out of order."

Of course, that's just my opinion. I could be wrong.

sexual

harassment

ALL RIGHT, LET'S PUT OUR CARDS ON THE TABLE, we've got a dicey little subject this time around, Sexual Harassment. Now, it's pretty easy for me to come out on my HBO show week after week and do some high-concept screed about how, for instance, I think "violence is bad." Oh, well, thank you, Dr. Insight. But this week, we're crotch-deep in a good old-fashioned quandary, aren't we? The age-old battle of the sexes situated in the *au courant* Circus Maximus of the workplace.

Look, I should tell you right up front that while I'm sure many of you think of me as the world's most insightful hermaphrodite, I am, in fact, a guy.

So I have to confess that my first thoughts on this issue were, "Well, it can't be all that bad, can it? Certainly, a lot of these cases have to be trumped up, don't they?" But then I flashed on the fact that much of what goes through my head is shot through the dick prism.

Now I don't want to get off on a rant here, but what do I really know about what it's like to have some fat, foul-breathed, ham-handed boss leaning over your shoulder while you type, or laying his hands on your waist while you fax something?

I have no idea about how it feels to have some leering, pawing, needy co-worker breathing down your cleavage while you try to keep the best job available in a small town without much opportunity so that you can put your kids in clothes without the help of a deadbeat ex-husband. That has got to be brutal. So, thank you. Thank you.

So all I can really do is be honest with you, and myself, about what *I* have observed in my forty years of draggin' a penis around this pebble we call Earth. And that is this: I think men, more often than not, are probably guilty of a lot of the shit that they're being accused of.

From my observations, a lot of guys act so badly and so stupidly with women in nightclubs, and at the beach, and on the street, I know that if they got some occupational leverage they would probably use it as a come-on.

Why are men like that? Well, because over the years men have written a rule book—not all men, sit down, Donahue—but, many men have written a rule book that says it's okay to look the other way when certain members of the male herd squeeze, pinch, and demean women.

Well, now the rules are finally being rewritten. And as men and women go through this period of readjustment, the bad behavior is coming back to haunt us, isn't it?

Because nowadays we're hearing more and more stories of men being accused of sexual harassment and instantaneously presumed guilty until proven innocent.

But just because *many* men are guilty it is dangerous to jump to the conclusion that *all* men are guilty.

All right, now that we understand our game, let's introduce the duelists: Paula Jones versus Bill Clinton, *in* the Board of Education building. Do I think something hap-

pened between them? I most certainly do. He's a powerful man who also happens to be a tenth-degree horn
dog.

And you know something, I think most of you will agree,
once you get beyond all this faux-patriotic re-bop about
besmirching the presidency with tawdry accusations, the
fact is, Bill Clinton probably achieved emeritus status in
the Players' Club while governor of the state of Arkansas.
There is too much rumor, too much innuendo, and just
enough evidence. Bottom line, where there's smoke,
there's friction. You know, Stephanopoulos must be feelin'
like the guy that Louis B. Mayer assigned to accompany
Errol Flynn around town. Georgie, Georgie boy has
become a sexual Red Adair and it appears our good
President was sinkin' a whole lot a wells in the mid-
eighties.

But having said that, do I think he sexually harassed
Paula Jones? Hard to say, and here's why. She did,
in fact, receive several salary increases after the incident.

Whatever cheesy chicanery went down in that hotel room
it didn't seem to affect her wage-earning ability. I also
think it undermines her case a tad that it seems to be so
much about the money. Seven hundred thousand dollars?
How'd they arrive at that figure? What's that, a hundred K
per inch? You know something, there's a fair to middling
chance that ol' P.J. is a big-haired opportunist, propped

up by small-minded, politically thwarted enemies of the President.

Now, having said that the sexual harassment charge might be specious, do I think that Paula Jones might have been compromised by the clumsy, sophomoric sexual advances of a presumptuous Huey-not-so-Long type lording his power over a backwoods empire?

Yes I do. Do I think that Paula Jones could have been embarrassed by the highest elected official in her state doing a Lurch impression with his Dockers down around his ankles? Yes, I do. But I would say this to Paula Jones—the next time a man drops his chinos in front of you, look him in the eye and say, "Listen, you silly son of a bitch, pull your pants up and start thinking with your big head for a change, okay, pal?"

Look, nobody wants to make light of the serious crime against women that men commit far too often. But isn't that what frivolous complaints like Paula Jones' are doing? We've got to get clear with each other on how our respective gender tribes wield sexuality in this culture. Because some of this stuff should be a no-groiner.

Here are some guidelines. To the women who are ready to haul the bag boy at the Safeway into court because he complimented them on their culottes, take the extra second and try to differentiate the innocuous from the malicious.

And to all the men who don't get the fact that when she says no, she means no. Well, I'm telling you, Quest for Fire boy, she means no!

Okay, it's over. Pack up your encyclopedias and go knock on the next fuckin' door.

Let me also advance the following immodest proposal so we can all get on with our goddamn lives; I think we should pour all our time, energy and know-how into genetically engineering a third sex that we can both fuck indiscriminately and never feel the need to phone the next morning.

We could. Thank you. We could call them . . . Recepticants . . . and they would heal the world. And while this solution might appear silly, it's no sillier than what we're doing now, which is a tentative, sexual two-step in which neither partner wants to lead, neither partner wants to follow, and everybody's feet are getting stepped on.

Of course, that's just my opinion. I could be wrong.

is

intelligence

a

liability?

ABC NEWS SPENT A FULL HOUR OF NETWORK PRIME
time last year talking to Michael Jackson and Lisa
Marie Presley. Why does something completely in-
ane like that fascinate us? Our culture has gone
from "The G.E. College Bowl" to the guy on
"Wheel of Fortune" who asks "Is there an F as in
pharaoh?"

Is intelligence a liability nowadays? I think we can answer that with one word: DUH. America's never been what you would call highbrow, but these days it seems our collective cranial ridge is sloping like the shoulders of the bar boy at the Kennedy compound.

Now I don't want to get off on a rant here, but we live in an era and a time when calling someone an Einstein is considered to be somewhat of an insult.

Morons are out there in force, making left-hand turns from right-hand lanes, trying to pay for drive-through tacos with a fucking check, calling 411 to get the number for Information. In most of our fine metropoli, the riposte "fuck off" will get you a seat at the local Algonquin round table.

What happened? I'll tell you what happened. First and foremost, as a matter of fact, numbers one, two, and . . . what comes after two? We didn't pay enough attention to our education system. We've got to stop paying teachers like the kid who delivers "Grit." You know, these . . . for Christ's sake, these are the people who will lead us and our children into the next century and they can't even afford real Yodels, okay, they have to get the 144-count price club steamer-trunk size of the Little Debbie's or the equivalent.

High school kids are entering the job market with an education that barely qualifies them to run the tilt-a-whirl at the traveling carnival. Even those fortunate enough to graduate from Ivy League schools, well, they go on to write movie scripts about guess what, stupid people.

And that brings us to our next reason. Let's face facts. The TV beast ate us, whole, quicker than a dog on a Dreamsicle, all right. Most talk shows are just Bimbomercials. Connie Chung actually hosted a network news show for a year. And many sitcoms need two longshoremen with a pipe wrench to twist the canned laughter dial. Bright people whom I really used to respect now stay home to watch "Beverly Hills, 90210." Why bother? You just know that every week Brandon and Dylan are going to let Kelly jerk them around while Donna and Ray are having yet another abusive spat at the Peach Pit. Ohhh, I *hate* Ray!

TV—TV producers say "Americans enjoy the stupid shit." But hey, it's the same reason Eskimos enjoy blubber—it's the only fuckin' thing available in the Arctic buffet, okay.

Pop—Pop culture has turned the brain into the body's new appendix—no real function, and it could quite possibly blow up and kill you. As organs go, you just don't need your brain anymore!

As a matter of fact, I'm certain in the very near future, people will go to the hospital, or should I say turn on the Hospital Channel, and get their brains taken out, just as a precaution.

Indeed, in the business of television, brightness can often be taken from you and used as the scimitar to cleave your occupational head off. Talk show host Jon Stewart ran a pretty tidy and, might I add, a pretty intelligent little Keebler tree over there, till it was chopped down last year. Now, there are many reasons for the cancellation of a television show, and I'm pretty sure Jon would tell you that the culpability flow chart on the demise of his show read like the genealogy of the kid on the porch in *Deliverance*.

But I'm reasonably sure it had something to do with Jon's use of words like "genealogy," which I think most Americans believe to be when Barbara Eden visits her ob-gyn.

America, we're at a fork in the road. To the left, you've got books. And to the right, the never-ending horizon of the new technology. I myself am taking a hard left, because if they talk you into hangin' that Rico, the new technology is only gonna make it worse. Now they tell you it's gonna make it better, but if you notice, the voice they tell you that in is always a computer-generated one and it's digitally synthesized, too. That means less work for us, less striving, less brainwork, more stupid, and eventually the King will be the one who just doesn't shit himself.

You know, our reliance on technology is making us soft. And if we're not careful, it will only get worse. Scientists estimate that by the end of this century, via the means of virtual reality, a man will be able to simulate making love to any woman he wants to through his television set. You know, folks, the day an unemployed ironworker can lie in his BarcaLounger with a Foster's in one hand and a channel-flicker in the other and fuck Claudia Schiffer for $19.95, it's gonna make crack look like Sanka, all right.

Of course, that's just my opinion. I could be wrong.

inefficiency

WHY IS IT IN AMERICA THAT GOING SOMEWHERE, buying something, calling someone—just about any transaction you can name in America is as nerve-racking as a Bosnian grocery run? Why is it that seemingly everyone with a job along the great service highway is an uninterested sociopath with the interpersonal skills of a wolverine?

Now I don't want to get off on a rant here, but why is it that I can't seem to go through the simplest procedures without a major hassle? For example, I recently sub-scribed to a magazine, and after paying for it they sent me another bill. So I called them up to rectify the situation, and they assured me they'd correct the problem. I then started receiving two copies of the magazine each week, one addressed to "Dennis Miller" and the other addressed to "Denise Miller." Now, I want to know two things: One, how can they not know they're sending two magazines to the same address, and two, how did they find out about my cross-dressing?

You know, nowadays, half the people you ask for help say, "It's not my job, man." And the other half don't have a clue about how in the hell to do their job. See if this sounds familiar: Hotel clerks who, even though you re-quested a nonsmoking room, give you a suite that smells like Denis Leary's index finger; maids who don't give a shit about the "Do Not Disturb" sign and come through the door like Pete Wilson raiding the kitchen for green cards at El Pollo Loco; movie ushers who constantly ask you to remove your feet from the seat in front of you, but refuse to even shine their flashlight on the gang-initiation golden shower taking place during *The Lion King*.

In trendy restaurants from the Upper West Side of Man-hattan to West Hollywood the one dish you can be sure is on the menu is *attitude*. Now I know all these waiters and waitresses have the talent to be the next Luke Perry. Or the next Luke Perry. Couldn't think of anybody else that bad. And excuse me for wandering into your restaurant in a quest for sustenance to jam in my pie hole. But from the time you strap on the Buford Pusser pepper mill to the time you drop your last check, do all of us hungry patrons a favor and use your sense memory to portray a wait-person who gives a shit about the customer they're serving even though that customer rudely insists on not being Mike Ovitz. Okay?

And it's not like I don't sympathize. I've been in the vast service gulag. After I graduated from college, one of my first jobs was as an ice cream scoop at a Village Dairy in Pittsburgh. I'm standing there at age twenty-one in a paper hat with my two fellow employees asking me if they're gonna find the driving test hard and the prettiest girl from my five years ago senior class walks in to order a cone. She recognizes me, and tries to cover her discomfort by making awkward small talk about sugar versus cake, as I think, "Yeah. I'll get laid on this planet . . . sure."

And once I had a job cleaning toilets for a living—on the *night* shift, for chrissakes. Got that? I didn't even rate cleaning toilets during the *day*. My bosses actually thought to themselves, "Yeah, Miller's good, he's *real* good. He's just not ready for The Show yet."

I know jobs can be unrewarding, but I'd like to go on vacation for a week, call the paper boy, and ask him to suspend delivery during that time and not come back to nine newspapers sitting outside my doorstep, screaming to every lowlife in the area, "Yoo-hoo! Over here! Nobody home!"

I'd like my groceries in a bag that will actually contain what I purchased, and not open up like the bomb-bay doors on the *Enola Gay* as soon as my pickle jars are over the cement driveway; I'd like the universal remote I bought to change the channels on my TV and not shut off my neighbor's home dialysis machine.

And you know, while we are on the subject of inefficiency, why doesn't somebody warn you that the "stay hard cream" will short circuit the "auto suck"? Are you with me on that? A little too specific. All right, let go, walk away from it, it never happened.

More important, I've had it up to here with corporations pushing the fucking unions around. You know if you haven't been laid off by now you're working overtime. Companies are lean and mean. And so is the service they give you: lean and mean.

Still, a lot of the blame falls on us. There seems to be this notion that good, honest, hard work is something to be viewed down our collective snout. That doesn't make the workers at the bottom of the pole feel very good. Does it?

If you want better service, the next time you see one of those workers in an "employee of the month" photo at a fast-food restaurant, suppress your urge to make your friends laugh by ridiculing the guy as a dork loser with a bad haircut. Instead, why not seek out the guy who actually took pride in doing his job the way it was supposed to be done and thank him for dotting the i's and crossing the t's and making sure there is toilet paper in the stall and ketchup in the dispenser. Make that person feel good because he is the last thin blue collar line between a frayed but still functioning society and full-blown "We'll be there anytime between 8 A.M. and 6 P.M. or maybe we won't even show up at all, assface" anarchy. All right?

And let's grab the reins as customers. Don't stay on hold forever. "What's that? I should press one if I am calling from a touch tone phone? Hey, Hal, I'm pressing flash, 'cause I'm hanging up now and taking my business to a human operator!" Don't settle for fish nugget and the green spooge, turn the car around, go back, and demand the goddamn cheeseburger you ordered!

And lastly, let's get our pride together, go to the whip, and regain our position at the head of the socioeconomic pack!

How about less billions being spent on getting the war machine cherry, and a few more billions on tightening up our educational system. Forget the "moment of silence" in the morning, let's shoot for a moment of *science*, okay?

It's time we stopped looking up Japan's ass, and you know why? Because that definitely is "not our job, man."

Of course, that's just my opinion. I could be wrong.

victimless

crime

WHAT ARE WE DOING SPENDING BILLIONS OF
dollars trying to keep people's private lives in order? And I'm talking about legal-aged, consenting
adults here. Not kids. We obviously have to take
special precautions to protect kids. But what is
this Orwellian hang-up of ours of sticking our nose
into other grown-ups' affairs? What concern is it of
ours if some mindless stoner wants to spend his
life hooked up to a Turkish skullbong?

Now I'm not pro-drug. They obviously cause a lot of damage. But I am pro-logic, and you're never going to stop the human need for release through altered consciousness. The government could take away all the drugs in the world and people would spin around on their lawn until they fell down and saw God.

Now I don't want to get off on a rant here, but it seems to really enrage the vast cheese-dog and beer-quaffing nation out there when someone decides to waste his own life chasing down chemical euphoria. And I'm not sure why. Our displeasure with someone hell-bent on self-ruination through drug use seems really disproportionate to its direct impact on us. And as a matter of fact, we amplify that impact when we attempt to enforce unenforceable laws. It not only costs us billions but puts us in harm's way as addicts are driven to crime as a means to an end.

Why do we chase druggies down like villagers after Karloff? Let them legally have what they already have and defuse the bomb.

You know, I think the hysteria about drugs is oftentimes baseless, and this comes from me—a man who has never done cocaine in his life, although I did smoke dope upon occasion during my stint as a student at Oxford in the late sixties. And the war on drugs is more often than not fruitless and patently hypocritical. Be honest with yourselves, now, what drugs are the most dangerous to most Americans? It's a no-brainer—cigarettes and alcohol.

Those are the statistical champions by hundreds and thousands of deaths. And wouldn't you rather shoot a game of pool with a guy smoking a joint than a guy drinking whiskey and beer? Someone smoking a joint doesn't all of a sudden rear back and stab his partner in the eye socket with the cue stick, okay. He's too busy laughing at the balls.

And as far as harder drugs go, if somebody wants to shoot up and die, right in front of you, more power to him, you know. It's his call. And you know, the herd has always had a way of thinning itself out.

We aren't stupid people, no more than anyone else in the world. So why are we obsessing on habits that harm no one but the habitual, while we let real problems slip even further out of reach?

We seem to be willfully turning away from reality, and from logic might I add, to punish people who in many instances are doing an extremely fine job of punishing themselves, thank you. And in some cases, they're not even punishing themselves, but rather just following age-old spawning instincts that are woven as deeply into their brain as is their need to watch "Seinfeld."

Is there anything more fruitless than trying to legislate sexual behavior? You know, according to the law, you can't even get a blow job in Georgia. No wonder Sherman hustled through there.

And really, if you stop to think about it, who is hurt by the time-honored, unavoidable trade of prostitution? Only the guys who pay extra to be hurt. There is no sane reason to cling to this archaic legal attempt to curtail an activity that will be around until the end of time. You know, you could come back to this planet ten thousand years from now and Man may have evolved to the point where he doesn't even take in nutrition through a hole in his head anymore, but I guarantee he'd still be cruising Ninth Avenue and trying to get a knob shine from somebody named "Desiree."

What sort of perfect, *Harrad Experiment* society are we striving for, folks? One where you will be forced by the rigid puritanical mentality of your pinheaded, Gladys Kravitz neighbors into a tightly constricted, overly regimented existence? A life safe from the temptations, and rewards, of the flesh? Well, if that's your kink, go for it.

But for the rest of us, let's save the money we're wasting trying to regulate other people's private lives. If an individual wants to smoke a joint, shoot up, or munch blotter-like Tic Tacs and drop out, then let him.

Let's put the billions we're wasting on a drug war fought by fitness fanatics on steroids and three-martini senators rolling in pork back in the educational system. Let's free the courts and jails of lonely men and broken women who feel the need to buy and sell sex. Let's let the hookers and their johns have a safe building somewhere, off the

streets, inspected medically, and taxed up the wazoo.
Let's go on from there to tax liquor and cigarettes 500
percent, so that those industries can pay for safe, one-
lane, drunk-proof highways and air-purification systems.

Most important, let's stop pretending that people are going to lead the lives that we tell them to lead. Let's stop
pretending that a few simple prohibitions on substances
and activities will yield up a nation of Beaver Cleavers,
polite, clean, sexless, and ready to serve their fellow man,
no questions asked.

People are people. They are going to do with their lives
what they want to do, whether you like it or not. There is
nothing you can do about them that won't break the bank,
overcrowd the prisons, or corrode an already oxidized judi-
cial system. People are perennially going to continue to
get fucked up, and fucked, and we are going to continue
to get fucked over if we don't concede the fact that there
is absolutely fuck-all we can do about it.

Of course, that's just my opinion. I could be wrong.

activism

WE ARE A NATION OF PROCRASTINATORS, AREN'T
we? Activism in the midst of a passive period. And
that's a shame, because activists throughout the
years have been able to alter the course of history.
They advanced civil rights for African-Americans,
protected the rights of the worker, saved the
whales from being extinct, and once kept "Spenser:
For Hire" on for a whole extra season.

Now I don't want to get off on a rant here, but it seems the activism times, they are a-changin'. Increasingly, we've become such a nation of self-obsessed me-monkeys that most of us feel like we've done our good deed for the day if we pull over and make a complete stop when an ambulance passes. And also, the tone of present-day activism seems to have turned for the worse. There's nothing more unbecoming than somebody who's pathologically rabid about an issue that in the long run is cosmically inconsequential. To the overzealous, I say: Stop being so selfish and work your rage out in your personal relationships like the rest of us. Okay!

I'll be honest with you. There are times I'd like to shout, "Shut the fuck up and stop blocking traffic with your 'Save the Head Lice' rally, asshole."

Sometimes it's hard not to think, "Hey, could I please just eat my Cherry Garcia without some aging Vermont ice cream hippies constantly reminding me how bad the rain forests are doing?" Hey, boys, as far as the rain forest goes, does a bear give a shit in the woods?

But every time I go to turn my back on activism, I remember that in the sixties, a bunch of college kids brought about the end of a profane war and helped boot out a corrupt President. Activism got results —people felt empowered. The sixties were the "Us Generation."

The seventies, however, were the "Me Generation," and the eighties, well, the eighties were the "Me, Me, Me Generation," where cruel got confused with hip, serious with smart, attitude with belief, and the Mercedes emblem with the peace sign.

Now it's the nineties.

We've gone from the Red Cross handing out coffee at floods to Ricki Lake and the freak patrol blitzing Karl Lagerfeld's office and chaining themselves to the Poland Spring dispenser.

Now to me, Paul Newman does activism the right way. He makes delicious popcorn, salad dressing, and marinara sauce and then mentions in small print that the profits from this enterprise are going to charity. He sneaks it by you instead of ramming it down your throat, running his whole operation with a truly cool hand.

Remember, there is a fine line between activism and just being a pain in the ass.

But trying too hard is probably preferable to not trying at all. Believe me, we're all guilty of lying in the hammock, myself included. I'm about as societally active as J. D. Salinger during hay fever season, because quite frankly, it's a tad dangerous to get involved nowadays. There are forces of evil out there—powerful politicians, multinational corporations, Dick Clark—that would love for us to

become the complacent, blond Illya Kuryakin tribe from
H. G. Wells' *Time Machine*.

And does activism even make a difference at the end of
the day? Is there a happy ending? Well, hey, I'm one of
the more pessimistic cats on the planet. I make Van Gogh
look like a rodeo clown. And, with reluctance, I will say
this—when you get involved, most probably, it'll suck at
first. It'll be hard work with unclear results. But you know
something? So what? That is life in all its glory. Life is
not a movie. The right thing to do is simply get in the
game. The price of apathy is too high to pay . . . remember "We Are the World"? You want to see Dan
Aykroyd singin' again? If only to prevent something like
that from ever, ever recurring, please—get up off your ass,
put some goddamn pants on and some undies, and *do*
something.

Of course, that's just my opinion. I could be wrong.

funding

for

the

arts

NEWT GINGRICH RECENTLY SAID IT IS ABSOLUTELY essential that we cut funding for Public Broadcasting. I believe Gingrich made those comments on "The MacNeil/Lehrer NewsHour."

Why is it that the newly elected Republicans in Congress are so intent on eliminating the National Endowment for the Arts? Well, historically, thumbdicks like these guys shy away from supporting anything that has the word "endowment" in it.

Now I don't want to get off on a rant here, but why do we suddenly find ourselves locked in this pointless little pas de doo-doo over something called "arts funding"? The federal tab involved here is a lousy 500 million dollars—one five-hundredth of 1 percent of the national budget! That's less than what Clinton spends on 1-900 calls from *Air Force One.*

The trick is, art is subjective. It's like Mapplethorpe's bullwhip up the ass photo. One man's homoerotic statement is another man's unfortunate incident at the proctologist's.

As a nation, we're becoming more and more leery of art, as if one whiff of a ballet recital will inevitably send us reeling into a depraved tailspin of nipple clips and amyl nitrite tabs.

You know, picking on arts funding is easy. Art won't ever find a cure for disease. You can't cut art down to build our homes. Art doesn't patrol our streets and protect us from crime. But then again, art doesn't hit us in the head with a fucking baton sixty-seven times. What art does is educate us, enrich our lives, and reacquaint us with the beauty of human potential.

Unfortunately, in the current Attila-like political climes, enrichment of the soul is the lowest form of plankton on the humanistic food chain. Conservative politicians may talk big about education, but they're cutting arts funding quicker than Sollozzo's capos cut Luca Brasi.

Face it, most of these politicos think PBS is what makes their wives so cranky each month. Oh, I'm sorry, I shouldn't have said that. I meant to say, what makes their mistresses so cranky each month. Besides, if we lose funding for public broadcasting, folks, you know what will happen? More fucking PBS strap-the-rat-cage on-my-face pledge breaks. Okay?

Believe me, it's not easy for me to stand here and defend the arts. I think that 95 percent of what passes for art in this world is complete and utter shit. And 4 of the other 5 percent is shit with an asterisk. But oh, that 1 percent makes you proud to be a human, doesn't it?

Come on, surely even you ultraconservative Republicans can sympathize with the empty feeling of watching true art disappear. You must have gotten a taste of that when "Hee Haw" was canceled.

Look, art is communication. If you get the message, or any message, it's successful. If you don't, hey, next painting.

So let's just shut up and bite this Lilliputian-sized tax bullet. Help keep some great old paintings and some deranged new ones in plain view of the average citizen, and at the same time, help defend individual expression against the first wave of the brain gendarmes. Because if we are to remain a truly great nation, we need to embrace our inalienable right to walk out of a modern art gallery, take a big bracing gulp of American air, and say, "You know something, honey? That really, really, really, sucked."

Of course, that's just my opinion. I could be wrong.

violence

LOOK, AMERICA HAS ALWAYS BEEN A VIOLENT
country—rent *Birth of a Nation* if you doubt
that—but nowadays we've gone off the Richter
scale.

I can remember when I was a kid leaving our
screen door unlocked at night. I can remember going to the playground and my mother worrying
about me getting hurt on the swings, not me get-

ting snatched and duct-taped into the trunk of some loser's Trans Am. I can remember going to school and worrying that the two bullies—*The Only Two*—might select me for a quick ass-kicking in the hallway.

If today's schools are any indication, in the future our kids are gonna have to worry about getting shot by the fucking guidance counselor.

Now I don't want to get off on a rant here, but violence has turned the American dream into an Imax–George Romero film. Look out over the landscape and what do you see? You see a demented Toontown, filled with carloads of gun-wielding maniacs exploding innocent bystanders like cantaloupes at a backwoods turkey shoot. You see a twisted bizarro-land gone crazy on a lethal cocktail made with equal parts of instant gratification, self-righteous anger, and notions of entitlement. This country's a hotel room and The Who are in town, folks.

You know, in the last few years we've seen cops beat the shit out of a guy like a piñata. We saw violent retribution at the corner of Florence and Normandie. We've seen two spoiled Beverly Hills brats chase their mother down the hallway, reload, and blow her away.

We've seen a woman cut her husband's penis off and the jury could not make a decision. Didn't have enough data—

"Let's observe her for a while—see if she does anything weird."

So you put her in a state hospital for six weeks. At the beginning of her stay you count up all the dicks.

Six weeks later you do a little Johnson re-tally. If the penal count is the same, she walks. It's the American way.

I'm telling you it's a madhouse out there. I feel like Heston waking up in the field and seeing the chimp on top of the pony.

How did it all happen? Probably too much wealth forming a thin crust over the poverty pie, too much of the good life on TV, and too little of it on the table.

But also, isn't the real problem here that somewhere along the line society took the wrong fork in the blame road and decided to give criminals the benefit of the doubt? How did they become the victims? Come on, everybody knows that's a bunch of shit, that's why *Dirty Harry* made Clint a big star.

You know it seems like we had some kind of handle on violent crime in the fifties, but in the interim thirty years the eye has passed over and we are back in the bloody storm called human history. Bottom line, folks, for all our evolutionary bluster and braggadocio we are animals and we live in a zoo where it's turned into free crack night in the ferret hut.

We have got to pull a Dennis Rodman and start getting aggressive on the offensive glass so the bad guys know that their next violent act will most certainly be their last. It's the nonpunks versus the punks in a Texas cage match for the unified belt and we must not go gentle into that bad night.

Of course, that's just my opinion. I could be wrong.

political

correctness

I'VE HAD IT UP TO HERE WITH THIS "PC" SHIT!
Why can't we laugh at ourselves? Why, when a
comedian does a joke on anything even vaguely
controversial, do certain people moan like somebody let one rip during an audience with the
Pope? I mean, come on, who actually moans at a
joke? Who is responsible for that? Well, quite
frankly, I'm pinning it on the gays, okay.

Now, now, I know there's some reflexively irate homosexual in the crowd thinking, "How dare you, Miss Thing?" And what I'm saying to you is this: I think so little of the variations in human sexuality that I refuse to treat you like a Fabergé egg. You are part of the human collective. Come, join in our reindeer games. You too can be poked fun at. And that goes for the whole spectrum of special interest groups out there wandering the freakazoid Serengeti plain.

Now I don't want to get off on a rant here, but trying to negotiate the narrow straits of what's acceptably funny nowadays is like trying to navigate through the Sargasso Sea of plastic toadstools in the middle of a bumper pool table. I understand where political correctness comes from—a scant forty years ago, we were doing "Amos 'n' Andy" jokes on the airwaves, for chrissakes. We were barbaric louts. But now, suddenly, we find ourselves in a classic overcorrection, where we're all supposed to zip through life like some huge societal squadron of Blue Angels, flying six inches off each other's taste wing, never ever deviating even one angstrom. Well, folks, there are a lot of different aircraft careening through the social stratosphere, and we better start working out some respectfully independent glide paths right now, or it's gonna start getting real messy.

Why don't we start by letting humor serve as our guide? Laughter is one of the great beacons in life because we don't defract it by gunning it through our intellectual prism. What makes us laugh is a mystery—an involuntary response. If I could explain to you why Jerry Lewis makes me laugh when he's trying to be serious, and why he makes me straight-faced when he's trying to get me to laugh, I'd have the answer. But I don't. But damn it, I'm telling you the key lies somewhere in Lewis! Yeah, Jerry is the "Stargate" on this. And I'm pretty sure, the comedic Rosetta Stone lies somewhere in his "catching the cigarette in the mouth" bit. And I think Charlie Callas will back me up on that.

The point is, people who are threatened by jokes are the same people who tend to refer to actors on the soap operas by their character's name. Listen, there's the real world, and then there's the joke world, okay. The joke world can get tough—wear a cup. When I watch Dana Carvey tee up his impression of me and how I run my hand through my hair, it momentarily irks me. But only for a second. Because I realize it's a joke, and I don't want to waste one more moment being angry when I could get back to my true avocation, which is completely idolizing myself.

Y'know something, folks, it wouldn't hurt if everybody held their cards a little closer to their vest. Don't let 'em know they've rattled you if it hits close to home. You should be able to take that joke right in the solar plexus, get up, get that two-cycle weed-whacker engine of a brain humming, and give as good as you got. And if you get bested, go home, sharpen your verbal machete, and get ready for the next thicket.

Don't call Gloria Allred Don't go to court. Don't steal a machine gun and shoot everybody at the party who made fun of your Jiffy Pop rag-hat.

Relax. Relax. The truth is, the human sense of humor tends to be barbaric, and it's been that way all along. I'm sure on the eve of the Nativity, when the "tall" Magi smacked his forehead on the crossbeam while entering the stable, Joseph took a second away from pondering who impregnated his wife and laughed his little carpenter ass off.

You know a sense of humor is exactly that—a sense. Not a fact, not etched in stone, not an empirical math equation, but just what the word intones—a sense of what you find funny.

And obviously everybody has a different sense of what's funny. If you need confirmation of that, I would remind you that "Saved by the Bell" recently celebrated the taping of their one-hundredth episode. Oh well, one man's Molière is another man's Screech, and that's the way it should be. But there are those who feel the need to enlist you in a cult whose core doctrine consists solely of *their* personal beliefs. Well, I subscribe to the theory of "The Cult of One." The cult of the individual. That way, if I "lemming" off the cliff, I'm only following my own nose and not the ass of another lemming. That's what America's all about. A great nation that guarantees you the right to lead whatever sort of existence you want to lead, that guarantees me the right to ridicule it mercilessly.

Come on, am I the only one who absolutely delights in the fact that somewhere out there near the pillars of Hercules there's a crazy old bitch like Marge Schott?

You know something, there's nothing wrong with a culture where everybody has a different idea of what's humorous. The last time I can remember an entire nation being on the same page, it was Germany in the late thirties and it didn't really turn out that funny. Remember: In its time and place, what Hitler said was considered politically correct; and it's that blind adherence to what is situationally palatable that is truly dangerous. We should question it all. Poke fun at it all. Piss off on it all. Rail against it all.

And most important, for chrissakes, laugh at it all. Because the only thing separating holy writ from complete bullshit is your perspective. It's your only weapon. Keep the safety off, don't take yourself too seriously, and remember that at the end of the day, this is just an ant farm with beepers, and it takes zero politically correct assholes to screw in a light bulb, because they are perpetually in the fucking dark.

Of course, that's just my opinion. I could be wrong.

race

THE TOPIC IS *RACE* IN AMERICA. NOW, RACE IS
touchy. I am so uptight about being called a racist
that I refuse to separate the whites from the colors
in my wash. So, let's proceed with caution. Everybody stay frosty.

So before we get started, I'd like to reacquaint
our contestants with some basic rules of the

game. Let's call it the National Race Aptitude Test. Ready?

QUESTION ONE: Of all the ethnic groups in America, which one did not come here voluntarily?

Answer? African Americans.

QUESTION TWO: All ethnic groups have gone through a period of social rejection, but which one recorded a lynching as recently as 1991?

That would be your African Americans again.

LAST QUESTION: On a national level, blacks obtained the right to vote waaaaay back when?

Nineteen sixty-five. That's right, folks. A mere thirty years ago we were South Africa without the diamond mines. And that's the end of the test.

Now I don't want to get off on a rant here, but let's face it, racism in America is growing faster than the lint ball in Chris Farley's navel.

Now, personally, I'm baffled by the concept of racial prejudice. Why hate someone based on the color of their skin when, if you take the time to get to know them as a human being, you can find so many other things to hate them for? I mean, come on, uhh, I mean, come on, jerks are everywhere, all colors, all races. All religions too. Just look around you and take a moment to notice, and you'll see more assholes than a Turkish customs agent.

Of course, it's reasonably ironic getting all self-righteous about racial and socioeconomic segregation here in Los Angeles. The inequity in this town makes Charles Dickens' London look like a kibbutz.

But you know, L.A. is just a microcosm. It's everywhere. The reasons—well, probably the main one is that people are increasingly overworked, underpaid, unhappy, disappointed, and confused. And when people feel they're being fucked around in life, they look for someone or some group to blame.

And you know the more America's multicolored tectonic plates adjust to relieve their strain, the wider the surface cracks become.

Fear and insecurity touch many nutcakes 'cross this great land of ours. Up in our Ivory Towers, white professors whose closest contact with real black people is James Earl Jones' voice-over on CNN are busy composing master treatises on the genetic deficiencies of blacks.

Meanwhile down the hall in the Afro-centric wing, a learned Ph.D. in mathematics is insisting that X = Malcolm.

And down at street level, we've got an eclectic little menu of cross-burnings, drive-bys, quotas, and people crying racism in lieu of wolf. Welcome to 1995, can I take your coat?

So what's the solution?

Maybe a nice first step in the healing process would be to take stock of where we currently stand. I believe the different races in this country are making progress. Slow progress, yes, but real progress.

Nonetheless, we should probably all take time off from our incessant self-flagellation, count all the ingredients we have for a massive full-blown racial donnybrook, and marvel at how wonderfully we *do* actually get along.

Maybe we could also get a little less whiny about the slings and arrows of people whom we should not give one tenth of one shit about. Why should I or you give somebody else—somebody who doesn't even *know* us as a person—the power over whether we feel good about ourselves or not?

To those who would try to diminish us, or anybody else, based on melanin content or lack thereof, I say this: My self-opinion is decided by fiat, not consensus, and I'm sorry, but the polls are closed and I'm afraid you're no longer eligible to vote.

Also, it's nice we all came from somewhere, but we are here now and it's time to be proud of America. We're living in a melting pot, so melt, for chrissakes.

Hey, I'm not a Pollyanna about the way the world works. Not all the turtles are going to make it to the ocean. That's not negativism, that's pragmatism.

But if you do find yourself on your back around four feet away from the water with some six-year-old kid from Redondo Beach shoving an M-80 up your turtle ass, don't blame another group of people for your shitty life. Get *your* life together and fight to reach the breakers.

Listen, I'm talking to every honest, sane, good-hearted person out there, whether they are black, white, brown, yellow, red, green . . . okay, if you're green, go back to where you came from. All right. That's where I draw the line: The point, the point is why in the hell are we letting the clown acts run the fucking circus in this country?

Hate is an excuse.

Somehow, some way, we've got to find the courage to love the hate-filled extremists on both sides, to connect with them, to disperse the rage, to tell them that it's time to come in from the embittered cold and join in our Rainbow-hued Twister Game.

Because the main thing I want you to remember is this.

If you think racism goes away when we're all one big happy color, with all the infidels weeded out, well, I've got news for you, you're missing it big time. Don't you see, first you kill off all the other races, then you start killing off all the other religions, then you start killing off the left-handed people, then you start killing off each other over the length of your crew cuts, until finally there's only one guy left—and no doubt he'll attack the mirror.

Of course, that's just my opinion. I could be wrong.

power

WHAT IS POWER? POWER IS GETTING AN HONORARY
doctorate from the university that expelled you
your freshman year. Power is living in a mansion
for thirty years and never exactly knowing where
the kitchen is. Power is walking around with your
fly open and everybody thinking you're a fashion
leader. Power is the most sought-after, addictive,
seductive, abused drug there is. Compared to
power, crack is Fruitopia.

I'll wager that human beings fantasize more about power than they do about anything else: wealth, fame, making the winning play for their favorite team, leg-wrestling Rue McClanahan . . . her strong, support-stockinged calves pressing firmly against my . . . I'm sorry, where were we? Oh, right, power.

I believe it's the Bible that says, "With great power comes great responsibility." No, wait, that was Stan Lee in "Spiderman."

Now I don't want to get off on a rant here, but let's talk about power—how to get it, what to do with it, when to use it, and most importantly, where to store it at what temperature. Because make no mistake, power is a perishable good.

Now, I may currently appear to have power, but if you really think about it, I'm just a mindless fuck chimp for HBO. At any moment, they could back up a costume van, pull out the Pillsbury Doughboy suit, and order me into it, and then what? Well, nothin' says good lovin' like something from the oven . . . teeheehee . . . that's what. At the end of the day, I've got all the power of that highway construction worker who can't be trusted with any moving-part machinery 'cause he took a crane hook to the temple in '89, and changed his name to Slappy, and now he has to stand there all day with a reversible sign that says "Stop" and "Go," until the weekend, when his friends invite him to parties and make him dance by shooting pellet guns at his feet.

So while I obviously don't have it, who does? Well, let's define the different gradations of power. First, there's real power—a tornado ripping up a hundred-year-old tree and picking its teeth with it.

Then, there's real human power—high-grade political power. At the top of this heap, it is a pure, uncut, China White House jolt right into the arm that has its finger on the button. You think Clinton doesn't like the power of being President? You think he doesn't sit there in the Oval Office for hours saying to himself, "This is the finger that could blow up the world and it's the same finger I use to scratch my ass with."

Next, you have mid-range corporate power—that flawless, synergistic weaving of money and clout that allows a se-lect few to meet in smoke-filled backrooms and literally change the course of human history while the rest of us are waiting in line for a kid to ask, "Do you want fries with that?"

And finally, there's pretend power, the supposed ability of one person to lead a flock of sheep to new heights, where, unfortunately, they usually find a shearing pen. Who has this power? Jimmy Swaggart, Amway, Dionne Warwick, Barney, Rush. How'd they get it? Well, you gave it to them, for chrissakes. Stop doing that. Go to Starbucks, get a quadra-latte, and wake the fuck up.

So those are the different kinds of power. The only other thing you need know is that we all crave power. Whether it's heading a major entertainment company or just spraying that cockroach in your kitchen with a steady stream of Raid and pretending you're Red Adair on a blazing oil platform in the middle of the Caspian Sea.

Face it, we all get off on power. Even if we only have a little of it. You think that clerk at the DMV doesn't enjoy looking at that snaking line and thinking, "I gotta be here eight hours? Well then, you gotta be here eight hours."

Power is the nutritional source that feeds the ego. And of course we all know that the ego is the ugly little troll that lives underneath the bridge between your mind and your heart.

If you keep a stranglehold on that fact, I don't think the desire for power is necessarily a bad thing. I'd say it's encoded into our DNA for a damn good reason. After all, back in the prehistoric days when we humans dwelt in caves and the neighbor's raptor got off its leash and shit in your yard and then ate your cave son, you sure as hell needed a big stick. You couldn't go running to Johnnie "Rockran," or whatever they called the neighborhood's ultra-smooth bullshit artist back then.

So, to all of you out there constantly whining about how to get power, well, you can start by not giving any of yours away. Don't send twenty bucks to some porcelain eyeliner junkie who claims she can get you into heaven. That chick can't even get you into Costco. There's only one guy who can get you into heaven, and that's God . . . or Buddha, or Eisner, or whatever the hell he's calling himself these days.

Of course, that's just my opinion. I could be wrong.

contemporary

sports

THE WORLD OF SPORTS COULD USE A SHOT IN THE arm, couldn't it? I bought a newspaper the other day. I was gonna flip to the sports section when I realized, I just can't make the Mark Belanger–like throw from the hole anymore. I just don't want to read about vicious brawls, random drug testing, salary squabbles, or venomous court proceedings. For chrissakes, it's enough to make you wanna go to the front page.

Now I don't want to get off on a rant here, but I remember as a kid thinking sports were played by heroes on a field of honor. We played on our little neighborhood sandlots in hopes of someday becoming the noblest of all warriors: a ballplayer. Today I can see ballplayers for what they are—just young men with a bag of faults covering the whole spectrum of human frailty.

On the baseball cards of my youth, collected assiduously and filed in an empty Converse sneaker box, the boys of summer smiled white smiles, their eyes clear and happy with the sense of purpose that comes from honorable pursuits. They were our *team*. They stayed with us through good and bad and they didn't hold out for more money, and we didn't withhold our adulation.

There was a predictability to the equation then that was, in one word, comforting. The plotline read as simply as a *Spy vs. Spy* comic strip. Young man works hard, plays fair, becomes hero, gives back to fans, and rides off into the sunset. Nowadays, young man squirts bleach at reporters, throws firecrackers at kids, becomes felon, and drives Porsche off into sunset. You know, the equation doesn't work anymore.

The math now dictates that Bonnie Blair trains hard, keeps her mouth shut, wins five gold medals—*five*—and she can't get a headband endorsement. Nancy Kerrigan comes in second—*once*—tells Mickey Mouse to go fuck himself, and she strikes the mother lode.

You know, just like all other walks of society, sports fame has become a matter of smile over substance. And you know, it's *all* sports.

In football, it's Jerry Jones' swelled head. In basketball, it's Dennis Rodman's mood-ring head. In boxing, it's Don King's troll-doll head. And in tennis, it's Andre Agassi's balding head. Yeah, we noticed, Andy. Well, you know something? I say off with their heads. They're our games and we want them back.

We are being cheated. The Four Horsemen of the Apocalypse are no longer Stuhldreyer, Miller, Crowley, and Layden but rather Greed, Ego, Arbitration, and Steinbrenner. The Elysian athletic fields of my youth have been turned into the Poulan Weed Eater dust bowls of today. The true poetry of sport has been corroded and we are left with nothing but the following broken verse.

It looked extremely rocky for the L.A. nine that day;
The score stood two to four, with but an inning left to
  play;
So, when De Shields died at second, and Butler did the
  same;
Bad karma clouded the Blu-Blockers of the patrons at
  the game.

A few got up to do some blow, leaving there the rest;
With that hope which springs eternal within the siliconed
  breast;

For they thought: "If only Darryl could get a whack at
   that . . ."
They just might put their sushi down, with Strawberry at
   the bat.

But Piazza preceded Straw-man, and likewise so did
   Wallach;
And the former was still three years shy of arbitration,
   and the latter was a five-and-ten man who was
   contractually guaranteed final approval of the teams
   he could be traded to;
So on that earthquake, brushfire, mud slide, riot-torn
   Angelyne-billboard stricken multitude, a deathlike
   silence sat;
For there seemed but little chance of Darryl getting to
   the bat.

But Piazza let drive a "triple," to the wonderment of all;
And the inconsistent Wallach took a slider in the balls;
And after his obligatory charge to the mound to make his
   feelings heard;
There was Wallach safe at first, and Piazza a-huggin'
   third.

Then from the jaded multitude went up a wine spritzer–
   soaked yell;
It rumbled off the 405 and the Hollywood sign, as well;
It struck off Spago's windows, which shook like
   liposuctioned fat;
For Darryl, flighty Darryl, was advancing to the bat.

There was disease, Lasorda would say weakness, in
Darryl's manner as he twelve-stepped into place;
There was pride in Darryl's bearing and some white stuff
on his face;
Sixty thousand and one eyes were on him—okay, Peter
Falk was there, it's Hollywood—as he rubbed his
hands with dirt;
Thirty thousand folks applauded, dripping DoveBars on
their shirts.

Now the leather-covered sphere came hurtling through
the smog;
And Darryl stood a-watching in a self-indulgent fog;
Close by the useless batsman the ball unheeded sped;
"I've seen better orbs at strip clubs," said Darryl. "Strike
one," the umpire said.

From sky boxes stuffed with Armani suits there went up
a muffled roar;
Like the whacking off of perverts in that park on the
Santa Monica shore;

Hey, I was looking for a rhyme.

"Kill him! Kill the umpire!" shouted Kevorkian in the
stands;
And it's likely they'd have killed him, had not Darryl
raised his spouse-abusing hand.

He signaled to the pitcher, and once more the spheroid
flew;

But Darryl had nearly nodded off, and the umpire said,
    "Strike two."

"You suck, you worthless piece of shit," cried the
    maddened thousands,
Clustered around my four-year-old son and me;
And then the echo answered: "¡Tú chupas, tú bueno pa'
    nada pedazo de mierda!"

But one scornful look from Darryl and the fans' inner-
    child anger cleared;
They saw his face grow stern and cold, like the day
    he smacked that homeless guy for lookin' at him
    weird;
Then they heard him whining about his 4 million per
    annum strain;
And knew that the chances were 2-in-10 he wouldn't let
    the ball go again;

And now the obscenely overpaid 8-and-13 pitcher holds
    the ball, and now he lets it go;
And now the shitty L.A. air is shattered by the farce of
    Darryl's blow.

Well somewhere in this troubled land the sun is shining
    bright;
The Eagles have reunited, and somewhere hearts are
    light;

Somewhere men are laughing, and somewhere children shout;
But there is no joy in Mudville: Mighty Darryl is strung out.

Of course, that's just my opinion. I could be wrong.

homeless

HBO HOLDS AN ANNUAL HOMELESS BENEFIT,
"Comic Relief." HBO's been involved in the homeless problem for years, probably because undoubtedly they have a sense of compassion and hey, let's face it, somebody doesn't have a home, somebody doesn't have cable.

Now I don't want to get off on a rant here, but the "trickle of souls who fall through society's cracks" has become a full-fledged tsunami. Have you taken a stroll around Manhattan lately? The only thing separating it from Calcutta is the Benetton stores. And it is a sight that's become all too familiar here in L.A. as well.

We've all seen them—wandering the streets with their possessions in shopping bags, muttering to themselves as they pick through garbage bins. But enough about agents.

Now, right up front, uhh, do I believe that every single one of these people that I see on the street has been fucked around by life? No I don't. There are some people out there who I think are scam artists, and I don't have much compassion for some of these seemingly able-bodied mid-twenties, vaguely threatening, attitude-laden guys who have decided that their personal statement is that they're going to give up on life at a very early stage of the game. Sorry, boys, life *can* be a mother-fucker.

And some of you just gotta get a little tougher. All right?! But importantly, I also believe that the great majority of people I see walking the streets are in trouble.

But the homeless are made up of many people—poor alcoholics, runaways, Viet vets, castoffs from mental institutions, immigrants, they're all out there every night. And the rest of us are finding it easier and easier to rationalize their plight. But there's one group of homeless people that we can't rationalize away, one specific sub-group that haunts us to an ever-increasing degree, the one that really rattles our thorax, and those are the unlucky.

People who couldn't quite cut a mortgage payment, got laid off a month later, had to leave their home, kid got sick, medicine wiped out the rent money, and wham, they're on the street. Even the assholes among us can't rationalize them away—Lazy? Stupid? Drunk? Drugged? No. They're *us*. They're us with one lousy fucking wrong turn somewhere down the line.

Of course, Rush Limbaugh and his ilk think the homeless are just the weakest of the herd who should be sent off to The Island of Misfit Toys without a pang of remorse. Ironically enough, Limbaugh is very popular with the homeless community in this country, 'cause there always seems to be a new refrigerator box in his trash bin.

And Limbaugh begat Gingrich and his congressional ilk, who are hard at work trying to pass legislation that would fund their new Stealth Homeless project. You know they're there, but you can't see them.

But for those of us not hypnotized by talk radio or partisan hype, we know a hell of a lot of people are living one paycheck away from being out on the street. There is no job security anymore. Most of the jobs available in this country won't earn you enough to pay rent on

Baltic and Mediterranean. And they're the shitty purple ones.

What's the solution? Is it too simplistic to say that karma dictates Kato Kaelin begin taking homeless people in?

Nobody has gotten this much ink off not having a place of his own since Jesus Christ.

And the answer certainly is not housing projects. Look at our most famous example of public housing—the White House. The government can't even stop the President from being shot at, how are they gonna do it for a group of five-year-olds in Cabrini-Green? We tried to come up with a simple solution to a complicated problem and ended up creating so much bureaucratic red tape we got caught with our panacea down around our ankles.

We can also disregard the suggestions of the ultra-conservatives that we should build softer sidewalks, or the ultraliberals that the homeless should unionize.

This is not about the right or left wing, but about the gated communities and the cardboard Hiltons. And if many of the people on the streets *are* mentally ill, well, a lot of people in houses are, too. You just can't keep tinting your car windows until you can no longer see your beleaguered neighbors out on the street.

Folks, there are so many things we don't have the cure for, but *this is not one of them*. When it comes to homelessness, we have the Lorenzo's Oils. Is there a greater irony than a homeless person sitting on the steps of a boarded-up apartment building? There are a shitload of buildings all across this country that are not being used to their maximum efficiency, and I'm not just talking about the Capitol Building.

We have to retrieve these buildings from building code bullshit-land and start making sure people without a roof over their heads are getting into them at night. No American should ever have to live in a dwelling where the walls read, THIS END UP.

In addition to making use of these buildings, we have to devise a system where the money donated to help these people goes directly into their frost-bitten hands instead of going to people who don't even need it. This country has so many special interests sucking off the entitlement teat that oftentimes the only substantive money actually getting through to the homeless *is* in the form of spare change.

And finally, what we have to understand as a nation is that Thomas Jefferson didn't quite go far enough—all men are created equal, but not all men are equal at all times. And occasionally, people need assistance. They have trouble keeping up with the pack, and while it might be difficult, if we can't begin to make the wide bank and swing this *Love Boat* around so that we can go back and throw life preservers at nonswimmers drowning in our wake, then we truly deserve to hit a fucking iceberg.

Of course, that's just my opinion. I could be wrong.

women

in

hollywood

OH, COME ON, HOLLYWOOD HAS ALWAYS BEEN screwed up with its take on women. Look at the movie *Pretty Woman*. This was a man's view of prostitution—Hey, tool down Hollywood Boulevard about 2 A.M. some Saturday and try to find a Julia Roberts look-alike.

Now I don't want to get off on a rant here, but Hollywood is a mean little town. And I'll grant you it has to be unbelievably grating for women to lie back on the casting couch and look up at a glass ceiling. Still, everybody has to eat shit in this town—it's just some people get to write it off.

Hollywood does what it does for financial reasons alone. If Hitler walked into this town and said, "I've figured out how to do *Die Hard* in a hot air balloon!" he'd have a three-picture deal before you could say Carrot Top, all right? The liberalism of this town thrives only in living room fund-raisers and over expensive wines at Morton's and Spago. Watch enough television, see enough movies, and you'll realize that people in Hollywood will say or do anything to make a buck. They will decry the lack of women's roles in the same breath as they green light *Tootsie*, *Mrs. Doubtfire*, and *The Crying Game*.

Hollywood has always been a contradictory compost heap of rationalizations. The whole business of entertainment is a Janus mask hanging on an outhouse door—one face pious, liberal humanitarian, devoted to good causes and politically relevant art, the other face an avaricious Philistine willing to dress its own mother in spandex if it will help the ratings.

So if Hollywood will do anything for money, why would they exclude women? In fact, *do* they exclude women? Or do they just not *include* them enough to satisfy women?

I mean, think about it. How hard is it to find women in Hollywood? Name five great male actors. Easy to do? Pretty much. Name five women. Just as easy, isn't it? Holly Hunter, Meryl Streep, Sharon Stone . . . the woman in *The Last Seduction,* and, uh . . . Traci Lords.

I'm kidding, but the point is you instantly thought of ten other great actresses you wanted me to name—Glenn Close, Cicely Tyson, Jobeth Williams, Michelle Pfeiffer, Sigourney Weaver, Susan Sarandon, Winona Ryder, Dianne Wiest, Mia Farrow, Jodie Foster. It's a long list and I've left out a lot of great actresses. So what's the problem? What are women saying? I've got to believe the real problem isn't that there are no women on screen, but that women don't feel their essential nature is ever allowed on screen.

That actresses, as good as they are, as prevalent as they are, are still not allowed to be "women," not allowed to express a true, feminine point of view. They feel bound by the male view of women, to be either a sexpot or a shrew . . . a witch bitch or a Barbie doll. Or without men at all, on the run with another disappointed chick in a convertible. You know, it's man's simplistically polarized view of the role of women in the universe that women must find so frustrating. It's the Madonna/whore thing. No, I mean the psychological theory.

But the fact is, women are in Hollywood, in large numbers, on screen and off. Not yet equal, not yet as powerful as men, but getting there. The hard way, I admit, because no guy wants to be the first to say, "Hey, too many guys have jobs, take mine!"

But women will get there, and when they do, they'll make a movie that is about women as *women* see women. And *women* will release it into theaters, and the odds dictate that *women* will lose money on it, and, finally, *women* producers will be the ones making movies about sexpots and shrews in mortal combat with bullies and bastards.

I look forward to that, you know why? Because when women are free to be the ones who make the shitty decisions and give the go-ahead to make shitty films with vapid plotlines that you can see through like used Neutrogena, then and only then will true equality between the sexes have been achieved.

Of course, that's just my opinion. I could be wrong.

civility

HAS ANYBODY ELSE NOTICED THAT CIVILITY IS disappearing faster than a pack of smokes at an AA meeting? And you know it appears as if we've given up on trying to preserve it. Most people seem to accept this disintegration of manners as a *fait accompli* and have simply lined the borders of their personal space with razor wire.

Now I don't want to get off on a rant here, but we've devolved over the last few decades from a *Barry Lyndon* gentility to a bunch of Thunderdome mooks. Nowadays, thoughtless clods all across this great land of ours do everything from clipping their fingernails in restaurants to checking themselves for polyps in the buffet line. As a matter of fact, you can't go anywhere without suffering incivility.

You go to the mall to pick up a smoky-link Gouda gift set from Hickory Farms. You come out, your car's been keyed and some workforce fringe player has left a flyer on your windshield about how you can get 10 percent off gay porn films at Dick's Porn Film's Video Shaft.

You go to the supermarket and you wind up in the line that is clearly marked TEN ITEMS OR LESS, CASH ONLY, waiting behind a Ninja drifter with no ID, who's attempting to pay for fourteen fucking cartloads of puddin' pops with a personal check from the Bank of Tehran.

People no longer understand the basic rules of courtesy. Rule Number One: You must get out of the way and let people off the elevator before you can get on the elevator, okay? Rule Number Two: When you call someone at three-fifteen in the morning and get the wrong number, don't just say, "Oh, this isn't Charlene?" Click. Say, "I'm very sorry to have pestered you. I am an assface." And Rule Number Three: Turn your goddamn car stereo down—did you ever think that maybe I didn't want to hear the bass line to "Baby Got Back"? Did that ever enter your assface skull, assface?!

Even when I try to escape the cold, rude world, and isolate myself in a darkened movie theater for two hours of unencumbered escapism, I get stuck behind some idiot faux-Truffaut with my Anna Nicole Smith–sized box of Milk Duds.

But you know the fountainhead of all this bad behavior has got to be the daytime talk shows. What an intergalactic fucking freak show these are. You tell me, what Rusty the Bailiff Fan Club meeting do they go to to harvest these losers? Ricki Lake? Richard Bey? Jerry Springer? These people shouldn't be allowed to own a TV, for chrissake, much less be on it.

And you know their guests not only aren't ashamed of their asinine antics, they positively revel in their own grand mal shitheadedness: Screaming in people's faces, screaming at the audience, the audience screaming back . . .

I just want to say fuck this culture, pack up some jerky, and go time-share with Jeremiah Johnson.

Look, I'm not some tie-dyed karma maître d' trying to seat everybody in the no-conflict section. Day-to-day life, to say the least, can be combative. As far as I'm concerned, the New Age goal of perpetual, smiling bliss is a far worse hell than anything imagined by Quentin Tarantino on windowpane.

I don't want some vacant-headed, defanged Quaker land. That's not civility, that's banality. And I'm not talking Amy Vanderbilt civility either, where there's nine goddamn forks arranged around your dinner plate like some cutlery Stonehenge and if you choose the wrong one you're sent away to become Edwin Newman's personal sex-toy.

But you know, I am saying that when civility breaks down, the fall of civilization is close behind. Is it surprising to anyone that the least rude of all countries has 222 million guns? It's gotten so weird out there that we've all turned inward and in the process we seem to have forgotten there are other human beings schlepping this pebble. That's where civility comes in.

Civility is acknowledging that we don't live in a solipsistic universe. We do share this planet with each other, and we should strive to coexist in some sort of civilized, respectful manner. And so to all of you out there who don't cover your mouth, and who don't have the money ready when you get to the tollbooth, and who do burp so loudly in public that others wonder where the epicenter was, to all of you dwelling out there on the grassy knoll, if you don't want to join in this noble pursuit of good manners we are all cordially invited to, *please* . . . go fuck yourself.

Of course, that's just my opinion. I could be wrong.

criticism

BILL CLINTON IS CONSTANTLY CRITICIZED FOR HIS health plan, his tax plan, his choice of tie, everything. His haircut, his wife, you name it, some snippy bystander has an opinion. And sure, he or she is entitled to their opinion, but it's gotten to the point where people who criticize actually believe their opinion should have an effect, even if it's only that of birdshit hitting the driver's side windshield at sixty miles an hour.

Now I don't want to get off on a rant here, but why is it that every single activity in our lives is subject to a mean-spirited critique? Who wants to listen to some unqualified blowhard, having convinced himself that his uninformed opinion is somehow relevant, yarble through an insufferably long-winded, bullshit-laden rant . . . Oops.

Okay, I'm guilty here too, but having copped to that, I must say we truly are a nation of critics, sniping from La-z-Boys at a few active individuals struggling to effect political change, make a movie, write a book, tell a joke, design a better faucet—okay, *that* guy *is* an asshole. The faucets are fine, stop fucking with them, all right. The ones in airports are like science projects with the electronic eyes and motion sensors, water-saving springs— Faucet guy! *Stop it!*

Look, we used to keep this need to criticize bottled up in the Arts Swamp where it caromed harmlessly off giant soup cans, blank verse, and untalented exhibitionists smearing themselves with chocolate and cramming yams up their ass. But now, it's spilled over the media flood wall and into every activity of our lives: Sports, pet training, home repair, snow removal—you name it, somewhere there's a cable show dedicated to ripping it.

And I'm not saying there isn't a place for solid, intelligent, constructive criticism. But when was the last time you read a review of something, a movie, play, book, that gave you a real feel of what the author was trying to say?

It's probably been a while, huh, because nowadays you can only make a name for yourself as a critic if you pass out blow jobs like Madonna at the NBA All-star Game, or if you're a spiteful crank, heaping scorn on everything he sees, the kind of poison-tongued lard-encased asshole who *refuses to review* anything he *enjoys* because his praise mechanism was broken when his father wouldn't buy him an E-Z Bake oven for his tenth birthday.

Now I don't have any personal ax to grind here. Bad reviews don't even affect me that much. I'm not the kinda guy who names names—in fact, I don't even *know* the name of that slimy fuckwad from "Entertainment Weekly." But uh . . . I feel so cleansed . . .

The key thing to remember about all critics is that they remain dependent on the innovator, the person doing the real work of creating. And because they just sit on the sidelines of life, never the hunter, they are doomed to be forgotten. But it's not all their fault. I mean, we give them their chance when we rely too much on critics to make our choices for us. We give them the power because the sheer speed of existence has rattled our already fragile confidence when it comes to things artistic. We think we need help sorting out artsy things, that somehow we don't have all the facts.

But you know something? We don't need help! You like the Red Skelton painting? Buy the Red Skelton painting, all right? You like *Home Improvement*? Tape it and go over it like the Zapruder film. It's your living room, it's your life, go nuts! Enjoy the world on your terms. Follow your own heart and take what critics say with a fifty-pound bag of salt because at best a critic is just another human being like yourself, fumbling around in the dark, trying to separate the artistic wheat from the Wonder Bread.

So the next time you see Roger Ebert sitting there on his titanium-reinforced love seat, pissing off on the work of some young person who doesn't quite have it yet, but might be on his way to having it someday, remember the one time Roger decided to dive in to the deep end of the creative pool, he wrote the Russ Meyer film *Beyond the Valley of the Dolls*. And if you'll pardon me for putting on the critic's hat for a second myself, I must tell you that he was a huge, repulsive, quasi-radioactive, spectacularly inept, borderline-troglodytic pile of high-density, low-brow, can't get it out of your mind or off your shoe . . . Dog Shiiiit.

Of course, that's just my opinion. I could be wrong, and the balcony is now closed.

infomercials

I LOVE WATCHING THE BEAUTY PAGEANTS ALMOST
as much as I love watching the infomercials.
Thank God for infomercials. Seems like everyday I
think to myself, "You know, this fresh-from-the-tree
apricot is good and everything but, man, what I
wouldn't give to suck all the moisture and flavor
out of it, and dry it up into a wrinkled Asian beetle carcass!"

I can't tell you how often I've thought, "You know, I gotta learn Chinese wok cooking from an old, bald, Scottish midget." Or, "Isn't it about time I got hold of that exercise apparatus that shoves the seat up into my ass when I pull on the handlebars? I haven't been this tempted to purchase a piece of machinery since I bought the Craftmatic adjustable bed just to see if I could blow myself."

Now I don't want to get off on a rant here, but once upon a time, commercials maxed out at sixty seconds— simple messages from sponsors trying to squeeze in a quick word about Hai Karate before returning you to *Here Come the Brides*. But today, we have the infomercial, where commercials and information have been morphed, thereby violating the laws of both God and nature.

Salesmen no longer have to go door-to-door, or set up that little Ginsu hut at the state fair. Now they just slap on some makeup and shove their foot in your door via your TV. Talk about the right tool for the job.

They stalk us when we're at our most vulnerable—time slots that only Dracula and Charlie Sheen could appreciate.

That's when these "Sellivangelists" go to work:

Susan Powter. You know, the first time I saw Susan Powter, I thought Joe Piscopo and Annie Lennox had had a kid. A few years ago, Susan was just an obscure fitness instructor. Now, she's a well-known fitness instructor!

Mike Levey, the guy with the jagoff sweaters and the soft brain. Mike's more excited than a seventeen-year-old computer geek who's just downloaded some nude pictures of Courteney Cox off the Internet.

How about Ian, the Cockney knife-seller whose special knives can saw through a suspension bridge but still do delicate radial keratotomy eye surgery.

Dave Del Dotto. What kind of name is Dave Del Dotto? I thought that's the game you play in the casino coffee shop while you're waiting for your chicken salad sandwich. Dave Del Dotto teaches you how to cash in on property sold at distressed prices. Yes, people who had to dump their property because they went broke listening to Dave Del Dotto. I mean, come on. How much credibility are you going to give to a guy who thinks that John Davidson lends an air of integrity to the proceedings?

And the "celebrity infomercial hosts" are the kinds of stars you see on the "$100,000 Pyramid" and can't tell if they're the celebrity or the contestant.

And of course, we can't leave out the psychic hot lines. Just one question—How come the psychic hot line never told Dionne Warwick that her career was gonna hit the wall harder than Mr. Magoo playing jai alai?

And how come nobody over at the psychic hot line has a hairstyle chat with the 'Pubic Head" guy whose toupee looks like Barnaby Jones' ball sack in a tanning booth?

You know, only two guys did it right—Tom Woo, who advanced the theory that even the world's most unappealing Vietnamese cat could get bikini chicks if he was good with real estate. Woo understood that the simplistic, flat-line encephalograph American public understands only two things about real estate—that houses are green, and hotels are red.

And of course, the granddaddy genius of 'em all, the bull-shitter emeritus—Ron Popeil. The man who taught us how to tag graffiti on our bald spots. Now Popeil has convinced people there's no need to go to a supermarket to buy a 99-cent box of spaghetti when, for just $129.95 and a couple of days of assembly and labor, we can make a perfectly mediocre bowl of tagliatelle—in the comfort of our own cinder-block-based trailer home.

So if you're the proud owner of any of this *shit*, if you're one of those folks who really thinks you can get a better haircut from a fuckin' vacuum cleaner than from your barber, then wait till you hear what I've got for you . . .

It's an easy-to-follow three-step motivational system that will have you shedding pounds of politeness and tons of tact in less than fourteen days, or your money back . . .

It's called "Dennis Miller's Inner Asshole." And it works like this—you'll start with my introductory video, *Some People Are Fucking Idiots*. When you've mastered the simple "rude-imentaries" of that, it's time to move on to my advanced video, Everybody's *a Fucking Idiot*. This will help you trash anybody you want, *when* you want. And if you act now, you'll receive absolutely free my new best-selling book, *Fuck You and the Horse You Rode in On*.

But wait—there's more! I'll also include my audiotape, cassette, reel-to-reel, eight-track, or microchip brain implant, of 365 daily negations called, *Obviously You've Mistaken Me for Somebody Who Vaguely Gives a Fuck About Your Sad Little Life*.

So remember, that's *Some People Are Fucking Idiots*, Everybody's *a Fucking Idiot, Fuck You and the Horse You Rode in On*, and *Obviously You've Mistaken Me for Somebody Who Vaguely Gives a Fuck About Your Sad Little Life*, all for only $29.95! No, make that $39.95, and I'll throw in the Pocket Motherfucker!

Of course, that's just my opinion. I could be wrong.

what

women

want

from

men

DOES SIZE MATTER TO WOMEN? I DON'T KNOW,
what do women want? Nowadays it seems like
they want . . . other women. No, uhh . . . Some
women want zero from a man, others want lots of
zeros from a man. Now I don't want to get off on
a rant here, but I called up a female friend of
mine the other day and posed the question, "What
do women want from men?" She was genuinely
excited and began in earnest to address some of

the issues. That was three days ago. She's still talking. I had to pull the plug on my phone and cut the pole down outside my house.

You know, I'm not going to stand before America and try to speak for the female gender. I have only been a woman once in my life and I was young and drunk and in love.

Let's see, the myth is that women want Brad Pitt in the bedroom, Brad Pitt in the kitchen, Brad Pitt around the house, Brad Pitt during a game, Brad Pitt when they're sick, Brad Pitt in conversation, the body of Brad Pitt in *Legends of the Fall* combined with the voice of Brad Pitt, and to top it all off the IQ of Fabio on two bottles of NyQuil.

Another myth is that a woman must be married by a certain age or she'll never find stability. Hey, I've got news for you, ladies, looking to men for stability is like going to Crispin Glover for psychoanalysis, all right?

And yet a third myth is that men think that women like guys who are dangerous.

As a result, guys will often smoke cigarettes, drink too much, and ride a motorcycle without a helmet. Women don't like guys who are dangerous. Women want us to think that because women are trying to kill us.

And finally many of the myths between women and men concern sex. Sex is an area that increases the chasm between the genders. You know, it's insulting to her that you persist in going right to sleep after sex, and you resent that she dismisses your desire to have midgets film your lovemaking. If you want to know what women want in bed, it's very simple. Simple. Women are really not that exacting. They only desire one thing in bed.

Take off your socks. And by the way—they're not going to invite their best girlfriend over for a threesome, so you can stop asking.

But enough about all the myths. Let's get to the facts. Now I'll be the first to admit that men's advice on women is about as reliable as an M-16 in the mud, but this is what I kinda sorta, maybe think women want from men.

And this one's . . . going out to all the ladies in the house. Sorry, I just always wanted to be a Vegas asshole. All right.

ONE—Foreplay is not a privilege. It is a birthright.

TWO—If you take her out to a fancy restaurant don't try to subtly steer her away from the lobster, Diamond Jim.

THREE—Quit blowing smoke up women's asses about the sanctity and power they possess as lifegivers, and come up with some decent, affordable child care. That way, maybe poor single mothers can go to work and get off welfare and we won't have to listen to any more assholes in Congress blathering about orphanages.

FOUR—Equal work for equal pay. Look around you at work, guys, look around you at . . . Let's say Carl, the brain-dead jagoff in the cubicle next to you. You could kill Carl, couldn't you? Because he's a slacking, worthless toady idiot. Now imagine making 30 percent *less* than Carl. Hellooo . . .

FIVE—This is very important. During lovemaking: Don't ask, "Who's your daddy?" Even as a joke. All right? It's not funny.

SIX—When her mouth moves, pay attention, words could be coming out. Words are kind of important.

SEVEN—Pass a law that makes it compulsory for all over-the-hill rock stars to have women their own age in their videos.

EIGHT—Don't ask her if she *came*. You're a big boy now, Clouseau, you should know if she came.

NINE—Don't tell her how to merge, and she won't tell you to ask for directions.

TEN—When she catches you cheating on her and cuts off your dick in your sleep take it like a man.

So, guys, it's really not that hard. At the end of the day, when all is said and done, what women want from men is this—equal pay, fair treatment, respect, patience, sensitivity, passion, and a genuine effort at understanding who they really are. Or if that's too much to ask, how about a big fucking diamond the size of your head.

Of course, that's just my opinion. I could be sleeping on the couch.

freedom

of

speech

YOU KNOW LATELY, THE FIRST AMENDMENT HAS been absorbing more potshots than the west wing of the White House.

Now I don't want to get off on a rant here, but if it weren't for the First Amendment, I wouldn't be able to say, "Now I don't want to get off on a rant here." I'd just be some guy who works in a deli and says fuck a lot.

You know, the First Amendment reads as follows: "Congress shall make no law respecting an establishment of religion, or prohibiting the free exercise thereof; or abridging the freedom of speech, or of the press; or the right of the people peaceably to assemble, and to petition the Government for a redress of grievances." Wow, that is some tight, clean, sensible writing. This country was settled by people who did not want to be censored, who wanted the freedom to say what they felt. That's why they came here and killed the Indians in the first place.

You know as Americans we have a sacred commitment to uphold and respect freedom of speech, and that includes speech which we not only disagree with, but radically and fundamentally are opposed to.

Now, a Robert Mapplethorpe exhibit featuring a man with a whip up his ass may not be your cup of tea but it does prove one thing—some people will do anything to avoid waiting tables. You don't like Bobby's bunghole daguerreotypes? Don't go to the art gallery. Sure, you get upset if an artist displays a crucifix submerged in urine. But, what if . . . now, and follow me on this . . . what if it were a picture of somebody who didn't mind being submerged in urine? Suddenly you're not so upset, are you?

Folks, the last time I looked, my radio had a dial that changed the stations. If you like Howard Stern, listen to him. If you think he sucks, try Garrison Keillor. And as for TV, if you don't like what you see, use your remote control. I do. All the time. Continuously. I've got carpal-tunnel syndrome. Watching TV with me is like lookin' into a goddamn strobe light.

Should Andy Rooney be allowed to make homophobic comments to a newspaper? Sure. Is he right? Of course not. Should CBS fire him? Absolutely. Not for the homophobic comments but because that motherfucker hasn't said anything funny in fifteen years.

Sure, I'd like to see them stop airing the moronic bedroom secrets of dumb, fat, jerkoffs on daytime talk shows. I'd like to see them put a moratorium on movies that feature Harvey Keitel's dick—for God's sake, I've seen his dick more than I've seen my own dick. And I see my own dick a lot. And it's usually a pretty pleasant exchange. But, folks, that's the trade-off we make in this country.

Hey, you think it's easy defending some piece of shit movie I wouldn't watch on an eleven-hour flight to London with nothing to read and Martha Quinn sitting next to me? You think I want some farmer with a grenade pin for a brain blathering on about how the entire world is run by about five Jews from a luxury cave on Barbados? Well, frankly, yes, I do. The louder they bellyache, the better. Because then and only then—*we know exactly where these people are.*

We can listen to them and, God forbid, actually communicate with them. This way they can't ferment like bad yeast and ooze out of the brew vat when we're not looking. No First Amendment produces Hitler. Healthy First Amendment produces David Duke. There's a big difference there.

Folks, the only good thing you can say about banning certain books is it gets kids to read them. Stop wasting time banning things. The one muscle we should be developing right now is the one that helps us make the right choice. If some governmental bureaucracy steps in and makes those choices for us then that muscle will become weaker than a mixed drink in a strip club.

So the next time you get the urge to shut somebody up because they don't see the world exactly the same way you do, take a deep breath, get out your Bill of Rights, and count to the ten amendments.

Look at our latest censorship innovation for parental responsibility—the "V-chip." Now if you of your own volition want to install the "V-chip" on your television as opposed to personally screening what your children watch, fine. But anyone pushing for mandatory installation of the "V-chip" is hitting the mark with all the accuracy of William Burroughs trying to sharp-shoot a drinking glass off his wife's head. As far as that "V-chip" is concerned, here's a letter you should have tried first, boys—the "A-chip." After installation, it blocks out all assholes from telling us what to watch and how to think.

Of course, that's just my opinion. I could be wrong.

dysfunction

WHY DID JOHNNY FAIL IN SCHOOL? WHY DID
Johnny start hanging out with heroin addicts?
Why did Johnny get caught boosting stereo equipment? Why did he go to the big house? And why
was he released two years later and then appre-
hended with a Mannlicher Carcano in a hotel
room overlooking the President's motorcade
route?

Well, Johnny will tell you, in this week's *People* magazine, that his problems are all about the fact that when he was five years old he was in the school play, and, get this, Mummy arrived ten minutes late. You see, Mummy disempowered him. Mummy ruined Johnny's life.

Now I don't want to get off on a rant here, but thanks to the notion of the dysfunctional family, every zipperhead in this country can now tap themselves with the Freudian wand and in a flash go from failed frog to misunderstood prince. Tad tubby? Mummy mistakenly thought food was love. You say you're angry? Must have been your brother's midnight wedgie raids. Huh?

Or maybe you haven't fulfilled your sappy little junior high daydream about being the greatest person on earth, hailed by all, from the lowliest bootlick to the richest barons of industry—And you just know it would have happened if only your selfish parents hadn't totally ruined your self-esteem by obsessing on paying the bills instead of obsessing on paying attention to you and your silly, talentless antics on the diving board at the public pool.

Listen—folks, we all have dashed hopes, mere figments of futures crushed by graduations, jobs, marriages—reality. Sure, it's tough waking up from a deep REM delirium starring you as the focal point of the universe to an Eraserhead reality in which you're the condiment guy at Der Wienerschnitzel. But you know something, that shouldn't give rise to this shrieking cacophony of blame.

Every day we get a new escape hatch from the psychiatric community: Co-dependency, addictive personalities, inherited personality disorder, multiple personality learning disorder, no personality whatsoever disorder, fetal membrane subcutaneous infectious submissive sexuality dislocator, Epstein Roseanne Barr . . . for Christ's sake, we are going over a Niagara of psychobabble in a barrel full of holes.

We have become a country of ragged recidivists dedicated to the proposition that all parents are created equally bad and the progeny/progenitor dynamic should be the landfill for all our personal shortcomings.

And if you're deep enough in denial to actually think that you did have a happy childhood, then your shrink will tell you, you must be forgetting something.

"Think back, think back, way back . . . would some drugs help you remember? . . . Maybe a subtle question or two will help jog your memory, like . . . did your auntie Hortense ever make you take a bath with her? Did your own father ever put his mouth on your stomach and blow? And what for, if not to humiliate you? Sure, there you go, there's a good reason why your friends make more money than you.

"Hey, Jinky, you shouldn't feel bad about flunking out of school and getting fired from the trampoline center. It's not your fault. It all goes back to when you were an embryo.

"Don't you feel better knowing that all your problems were laid on you, man? All right, we have to stop now, Mr. Jinkelstein. That'll be a hundred and eighty bucks. And now that we know you have more personal baggage than Joan Collins on safari, I think you should start coming in twice a day for the next four Olympics or so because I need to pay off my Lamborghini."

Look, I'm not insensitive to the real victims of abuse, the human casualties of alcoholic neglect. There are people out there who have been dealt absolutely fucking brutal cards, and it breaks your heart.

But you cannot join that club solely through intellectual ledgerdemain. Let's be honest; too many unhappy, unfilled people see the bulletproof excuse of dysfunction lying there and pick it up like a cudgel to ward off any personal responsibility for their lives. And as long as we continue to allow people to make the easy turn and casually claim that they're victims, they will never even make the effort to Fitzcarraldo the boat over the mountain and achieve true personal victory.

Of course, that's just my opinion. I could be in denial.

fame

ONE WEEK, WE HAD ADVERTISED ON "DENNIS
Miller Live" that we were going to have Brett Butler from "Grace Under Fire" to talk about fame,
but she had previously turned down a discussion
of the same topic with Maria Shriver so she had to
cancel—because quite frankly she can't upset Maria Shriver because Maria Shriver isn't just Maria
Shriver anymore but a wing that's been added onto
the fame museum called Arnold Schwarzenegger.

You know, it's so weird to see a friend get famous and sink into the publicity-spin swamp. There they are, drinking champagne, posing for head shots, signing autographs, accepting a People's Choice Award, when suddenly— GLURB!—they disappear into the celebrity quicksand where you can't see them anymore—until they pop up on E! as the owner of the new Steubenville, Ohio, Planet Hollywood.

Now I don't want to get off on a rant here, but what is it that lifts one person out of the anonymous muck into the national klieg lights? It used to be that you actually had to do something to become famous—win a war, kill a dragon, right a wrong. Now what? You'll be famous if all you do is neglect your child to the point where she can tumble down a drainpipe. You'll be famous if you poke the local Drew Barrymore wanna-be in the workbay of the Levittown Long Island Lube-o-rama.

You'll be famous if, like Shawn Eckardt, you opt to have your boss's main competitor whacked in the knee with a pipe.

Does anybody remember when the famous fat man was Churchill, not some huge inbred Jabba the Hut bodyguard who thinks he's a fuckin' spy? You know, Shawn Eckardt's head is emptier than an Oktoberfest in downtown Miami. You know, when I look up at our cultural Mount Rushmore, I feel like Phil Collins watching

Ann Reinking sing "Against All Odds" at the Oscars. It is insane.

And here's the ultimate insanity. Two star-struck parents of a preadolescent proudly pack their son off for long weekends at the Neverland Ranch, even though the only thing they know about their child's thirty-five-year-old confirmed bachelor host is that when he's not having elective facial surgery, he's grabbing his crotch more frequently than Lenny Dykstra in mid-August.

What were they thinking?

Well, I'll tell ya what they were thinking. They were thinking, "the most famous person in the world is on the other side of that door, and if my child is the skeleton key that unlocks that door well then, so be it."

They were stargazing morons, and the man they were stargazing at is one of the five weirdest people on the planet earth, and the other four are his brothers. And you know something . . .

While we're on the subject, why do I even know Tito Jackson's name, for chrissake. Think about it. I say, "Tito Jackson" and you say, "Yeah, I know him. What about him?" And I say, "Exactly. What *about* Tito Jackson?"

You know, the irony of Andy Warhol's statement is that many of our present-day celebrities can't even fill the fifteen, folks, and we don't seem to mind. Why is that? Why is this country so quick with adulation for the banal, yet so begrudging with respect for the truly consequential?

We live in a culture where you can see the word "zeitgeist" pop up in a *Vanity Fair* article about Tori Spelling.

You know, all I can figure is that so many of us feel so anonymous, so powerless, and so insignificant that we howl and yelp at the mere hint of notoriety, like dogs watching the moon rise in the night sky. "Hey, forget the guy who saved the kid in the fire, when's Madonna gonna reveal her new look?" "Will the doctor with the cure for cancer please *sit the fuck down,* here comes Marla Maples!" You know . . .

Thank you.

Let's be honest, does anyone really believe that Marla Maples can "entertain" in any meaningful way? Does anyone think Marla Maples could even get extra work on a Spanish soap opera if her husband wasn't some low-rent Charles Foster Kane?

Of course, this is not to demean Marla Maples. Celebrity isn't easy. Not every silver cloud is a Rolls-Royce. There are always some people who just don't like you. You get on the cover of *People* magazine and two years later you see it in the dentist's office with your teeth blacked out.

You try your best to be your best and you finally make it to Broadway, then you step out onto a subway platform and there's a big poster with your picture on it, and some kid has drawn a dick and balls on your chin.

Look . . . in the penumbra between absolute obscurity and worldwide renown there exists a shadow region filled with a seething horde of pan flashers, egotists, dime store magicians and Holiday Inn cover bands hoping for a big slice of the adulation quiche. And while most of us are content to rubberneck the carnage on the berm of the road, too many people are desperately striving to actually *be* the car wreck, and I'm not sure we should feel compelled to recognize them.

Of course, that's just my opinion. I could be wrong.

where

is

america

headed?

YOU KNOW THIS IS GETTING ABSURD. WASHINGTON'S
blaming Hollywood, Hollywood's blaming Washington, and the rest of us are so zoned out on "Hard
Copy," "ER," and that new pizza with the cheese
in the crust that we don't even give a shit where
we're headed anymore.

Now I don't want to get off on a rant here, but
America has turned into one gigantic dysfunctional

family that's so far gone it makes the Menendezes look like the Von Trapps.

Look at our education system. Our kids have to pass through metal detectors simply to get an F-minus in woodshop.

And you know something, that four hundred to one student/teacher ratio is producing a generation of miscreant zombies who look at a mall map and think to themselves, "How in the fuck did the map people know 'we are here'?"

We're in danger of turning into a Beavis and Butthead theme park, a "Space-Between-Your-Ears Mountain." Within the decade, the odds are pretty good that we'll all be working for a thirteen-year-old Asian kid who's from a country that still gives a shit about education.

And what's the current status of our cherished, personal freedoms? Well, folks, we're the freest people on earth.

We have so much freedom nowadays that the President of the United States has to barricade the street in front of his fuckin' house just so he can scarf down a Moon Pie at midnight and not have to dive behind the Mamie Eisenhower ottoman. Great, we've turned Pennsylvania Avenue into a salt-lick for mimes. Christ, everybody's packin' nowadays. The other day, they caught Socks the Cat trying to yak a hairball at Clinton. We seem to be interpreting per-sonal "freedom" to mean stockpiling firepower that would make the Branch Davidian compound look like Ed Begley's place at Zuma Beach.

As for our much-beloved, two-party political system . . . well, right now, it's splintered worse than a jammed door at Chuck Norris' house.

The conservatives plan for the next decade is the inverse effect of "Back to the Future." It's essentially, "Ahead to the Past." Their plan may suck, but at least they have a plan. Liberals are running around like an organically fed, free-range chicken with its head cut off. No wonder they fight so hard for the spotted owl—they're right behind 'em on the endangered species list. Politicians better come up with something concrete soon, or our future will be *darker* than George Hamilton reading Sylvia Plath in the base-ment of a Mott Street opium den . . . and that of course is pretty dark.

And certainly our geopolitical gestalt has changed radically. Once we were a generous, outgoing nation, always eager to pick up a check or break up a brawl.

Hey, we were Hoyt Axton. Now we're on the verge of becoming the free world's answer to Travis Bickle—camouflaged, armed to teeth, and ready to off the first person who glances at us wrong. Our motto has changed from "E Pluribus Unum" to "What the fuck are you lookin' at?"

Sure, we're still the best nation on this planet. But does that carry the weight it used to? Nowadays, isn't that sort of like being the valedictorian at summer school? Given our amazing resources and our ideals, is this funhouse-mirror version of America really the best we can do? I don't think so. If America wants to bat cleanup in the New World Order, here's some common sense suggestions for moving into the twenty-first century:

ONE—Don't look to politicians to fix anything—get off your Snackwells ass and do it yourself.

TWO—Be open to new ideas. Buy electric cars when they go on the market. Sure they'll be shitty at first, but gas cars are shitty now. Get the shitty car of the future!

THREE—G. Gordon Liddy, shut the fuck up, all right?!

FOUR—G. Gordon Liddy, shut the fuck up. Just wanted to be sure, in case he just tuned in.

FIVE—Teach your kids about birth control so that we're not packed into these fruited plains like circus clowns in a Volkswagen Beetle.

SIX—Conservatives, don't censor Hollywood. It's supposed to be shitty trash. And what's left of you liberals, don't

censor Rush Limbaugh. Understand him for what he is—
a shopping cart with a bad wheel that pulls to the right
no matter which way it's facing.

SEVEN—How's about everybody getting their nose out of
other people's affairs and minding their own business? We
have become such a nation of busybodies and voyeurs
that the Constitution now reads, "We, the Peep-
Hole . . ."

EIGHT—Strive for a day when "NRA" means "Not Relevant
Anymore."

NINE—Try to keep in mind that for all the horrors and the
fear the media shove down our throats every night, most
people are basically good. They want just what you
want—food, shelter, love. We're mammals. We're migra-
tory creatures that no longer have any new places to go.
So now it's time to go inward, to do some karmic re-
tooling on ourselves.

And finally, the tenth suggestion on how to make America
a better place in the next century . . . stop ripping off
Letterman!

Of course, that's just my opinion. I could be wrong.

anger

HERE'S MY FAVORITE STORY OF THE WEEK. THIS
really pisses me off. Seismic studies show that
there's probably 1.5 billion dollars' worth of oil
underneath Windsor Castle. Well, it's good to
know that something over there's getting
drilled.

Man, 1.5 billion dollars' worth of oil and every
penny of it is going to the royal House of Windsor.

How unfair is that? More to the point—how typical is that? No wonder everybody's so angry nowadays.

And this is just ancillary nerf anger we spin off from the hard-core primal stuff that we all carry around like a venomous *Playboy* air freshener.

Now I don't want to get off on a rant here, but America is angrier than Burt Reynolds presenting an Emmy to Loni Anderson. We are angry that our streets have never been more dangerous. Angry at our so-called leaders for being more concerned with partisan mudslinging than solving our country's problems.

Face it, we are a PMS nation and have always been. Under the fancy patriotic paint job, America is a country built on anger. "What, you're not going to let us worship whom we want, when we want, where we want? Well, fuck you, limey! We're starting our own country! See ya at the bicentennial, assface!" As a nation we've been seething with anger from Day One.

But now this country is in the grip of a temper tantrum of cataclysmic proportions. At this rate we're only days away from having to install metal detectors in church.

Every little misstep in daily life, every minor tangle, every botched do-si-do, every burr on the dream of smooth sail-

ing is a potential interpersonal Gulf of Tonkin incident.
No sides, no cause, just sheer anger and rage.

You know, people are about to snap the minute they
shoulder-roll out of bed in the morning. They're still angry
about a dream where they didn't get laid. The snap factor
is so high you're liable to get beaten to death with a
canned ham in the supermarket just because your cart
rear-ended some frustrated, psycho, Ninja-wanna-be's cart
and you broke the head off one of his animal crackers.

And in America these days, that'll get you a Jimmy Arness
kung fu star lodged right in the center of your forehead.
And a jury won't even convict Grasshopper if the defense
can produce the decapitated animal cracker.

You know . . . Hey, it worked for the Menendez boys;
it's probably going to spring The Juice into the open field;
it's every bully's excuse these days, why not make it
yours? "Do I know how fast I was going, Officer? Yeah, I
do. I was doing a hundred and fifteen fuckin' miles an
hour because I have a huge red pepper of rage lodged in
my sphincter muscle." All right.

Let's cut to the chase. We're angry because we feel over-
looked, inconsequential, and undervalued. And when we
feel we don't matter it's easy to hurtle past the fail-safe
point, and we are gone; we can no longer be called back
by Strategic Air Command. They're impersonating our

wife's voice, and we're headed for Baghdad with the radio off and phasers on "Go Fuck Yourself."

And I, for one, am not apologizing for it. Why shouldn't I be angry? Living in a culture where MTV gives an ass wipe VJ like Kennedy her own TV show. Everybody feels anger. I don't ever want to *not feel* anger. But the collective mistake we're making is this: Anger used to be a bass line that we used to merely provide a funky bottom to our cultural zeitgeist.

But by not periodically adjusting our levels and assigning it its proper place in the mix, anger has now broken out into a shrieking Nugent guitar solo that's drawing a rivulet of blood from all of our ears.

This rising anger is the emotional head on a vast pimple of ignorance and fear. America is a melting pot of 250 million people who come from wildly different cultures, religions, and races, and all of them are feeling the pressure to succeed, to secure a place for themselves and their families. Being in America today is like being outside the gates of a Nine Inch Nails concert that's starting late, and the mood has turned from hopeful to fearful. The crowd has become a *Day of the Locust* mob. The jostling isn't friendly anymore; it's every man for himself. They just made the announcement that there aren't enough seats, it's first come first serve, and we're bracing for the big push.

We're angry in America because the fabric is tearing, the support rope is frayed, and the big gate is closing; time is running out and only the fierce little pig is going to suckle at the tit of plenty.

Of course, that's just my opinion. I could be wrong.

the

environment

YOU KNOW, I WAS DRIVING TO WORK IN L.A. THE
other day and there was some guy on talk radio
claiming that federal pollution rules are too tough.
I would have called him to argue but because the
smog was so thick I couldn't see the numbers on
my car phone.

Has anyone seen the Los Angeles skyline lately? I
think God invented the L.A. Basin so he'd have

126

someplace to stub out his cigarettes. And we all know the problem is not just here in L.A., it's nationwide. Hell, it's global.

Now I don't want to get off on a rant here, but we treat our whole planet the way college kids treat a frat house—we say we love it, then we piss on the stairs. There are so many oil spills our waterways are now classified "leaded" and "unleaded." By the year 2015, the earth's oceans will have a hard candy shell like an M&M. It'll be "Tupper-World." Eventually, every six weeks we'll have to burp the coastline.

And, as is frequently the case with human endeavors, there are two well-entrenched factions feuding over the environment, both convinced that their beliefs are sacred. But both sides probably aren't as far apart as they think they are on ecological matters. Remember—a developer is someone who wants to build a house in the woods. An environmentalist is someone who already owns a house in the woods.

But, truth be told, in a battle between corporate profits and the environment, the environment has about as much a chance of coming out on top as Pat Buchanan does of winning a "Soul Train" lifetime achievement award.

Will our politicians save us? Guess again, Woodsy Owl. They've already slashed the budget of the Interior Department, ended funding for environmental programs, and supported cleanup laws that are literally written by paid lobbyists from the industries that pollute the worst. When it comes right down to it, the green in our parks and forests will always take a backseat to the green in our legislators' wallets.

Where do I stand on the ecology?

Well, I don't want to sound like a wuss, but I'm somewhere in the middle on this one. I'm sure we all find it alarming that every year twenty thousand species become extinct and yet that Bronson Pinchot/Mark Linn-Baker piece of shit continues ad infinitum in syndication.

But then there's the flip side of this whole issue. Beyond ecology. Way out there on the fringe, we have the photosynthetically-crazed zealots—you know, the kind of people who jerk off to *The Hellstrom Chronicles*—the people who will tell you that virtually anything we do can wreck the quote/unquote "delicate balance of nature."

I have no idea what that refers to. From what I can tell from the Discovery Channel, the earth has traditionally been about as well balanced as Amanda Plummer on a triple espresso.

I mean, do we need to save every last goddamn variation of sandbug known to man? Do we really need the three-clawed hermit crab? The insouciant crab? The cable-installer crab? Fuck the crabs . . . and the seahorses they rode in on.

What we have to do is split the difference between utter disregard and paranoid concern and light down on pragmatic, well-reasoned, and, most importantly, attainable solutions. After all, we're talking about the future of our earth. The planet *all of us* call home, with the obvious exception of Bob Dornan.

So what are those solutions? Well, I think we all agree that the first step toward making this a greener planet is clearly, more songs by Sting.

But here are some other surefire recommendations to save the planet:

ONE—We need to all bite the Alva Edison bullet and reduce our power consumption. A nice first step in saving wattage might be to cut back on the number of digital electronic signs outside the Hard Rock Cafés alerting us to imminent problems in the ecosystem.

TWO—When using spray deodorants that contain chlorofluorocarbons, try not pointing it so much toward the ozone layer. We need the ozone, and currently, it has more holes in it than the plot of a Steve Allen murder mystery. Remember—the ozone keeps radiation out. The beach is no fun in a two hundred-pound lead muumuu. Unless of course, you're Alan Carr.

THREE—If you visit South America, don't burn down their rain forests.

FOUR—When you throw an aluminum can out your car window on the freeway, try to make sure it lands in a place easily visible so that the squares can clean it up.

FIVE—Get Hanna-Barbera to share the technology that allowed automobiles to run on foot power.

SIX—Petroleum companies, don't hire drunken freighter captains who'll inevitably end up spilling more oil around than Nick Barkley's barber. Christ, we're still paying the piper in Prince William Sound. If Exxon dragged its feet any more on that cleanup they'd look like Richard the Third.

SEVEN—Take your kids to an actual forest and not a theme park called Arbor Land, "where the trees almost seem kinda semi-real, don't they?"

EIGHT—Get rid of the mini malls. How many tanning salons-slash-do-it-yourself frame store-slash-manicure parlor-slash-Mailbox USA-slash-Taekwondo doughnut joints do we fucking need?

NINE—Recycle. Get rid of the mini malls. How many tanning salons-slash-do-it-yourself frame store-slash-manicure parlor-slash-Mailbox USA-slash-Taekwondo doughnut joints do we fucking need?

AND TEN—Let's all be adaptable people. There's always a compromise solution out there, if you just look hard enough for it. To all our friends in Taiwan—you guys like the taste of tiger penis soup? You think it's a delicacy, do you? Doesn't mean you have to kill the tiger. Use your heads. Just order a bowl of chicken broth . . . then have a tiger walk over and tea-bag his dick in it.

Of course, that's just my opinion. I could be wrong.

the

o.j.

trial

6/30/95

THE O.J. TRIAL. "WELCOME BACK, MY FRIENDS, TO the show that never ends . . . We're so glad you could attend, come inside, come inside . . . You're such a lovely audience, we'd like to take you home with us, we'd love . . ." Oops. Sorry. Got a little fucked up there, trying to be cool.

Anyway—to call the O.J. Simpson trial a circus is an insult to trapeze artists and bearded ladies everywhere. This trial has gone on so long, Robert Shapiro and Johnnie Cochran have shed three skins. See you moaned and then you applauded. It hurt, but you dug it. The pace of this trial is beginning to make me yearn for a PBS pledge break.

You remember when it began? Remember how we would gather, grape Nehi in hand, around the local television showroom and watch Detective Fuhrman's testimony on that tiny black and white Philco? It was a simpler—innocent time.

Now I don't want to get off on a rant here, but should this trial even be televised? Hey, I don't think O.J.'s performance in *Towering Inferno* should be televised, let alone his trial. But there it is on TV, bigger than Yeltsin's liver. Let's face it, television has given our legal system a skin peel, and the results ain't pretty.

We're all familiar with the cast of characters . . .

Marcia Clark has been analyzed more intensely than Linda McCartney's vocal tracks.

Christopher Darden is so disillusioned he'll probably leave the legal profession and roam the earth like Kwai Chang Caine from "Kung Fu."

The witnesses and hangers-on? Well, let's start with that waste of space and volume known as Faye Resnick, who was actually encouraged to crawl out from under her rock long enough to write a tawdry, self-serving mani-"fester" in the guise of an homage to a departed friend. Hey, Faye, how much silicone does thirty pieces of silver buy nowadays?

After her, we were stuck with cranky cleaning ladies who couldn't get their story straight in any language and a dishwater-blond professional roommate who only surfs other people's careers.

Kato Kaelin is to pull-out couches what Bruce Lee was to nun-chucks.

And the expert witnesses proved to be neither. Dennis Fung's testimony dragged on longer than the opera house shoot-out at the end of *The Godfather, Part III*. This parade of experts has got to cease. You know, folks, there are statisticians out there who can prove to you beyond a shadow of a doubt that George Bush won the presidential election in 1992. Christ, there's an accountant right now in Hollywood who can prove to you that *Forrest Gump* lost money.

And then there's O.J.'s much-ballyhooed dream team. Despite the fact that there's a mountain of evidence against O.J. that Anna Nicole Smith could hang-glide off, the defense team's big counter-argument is that it's a frame-up, a highly sophisticated police conspiracy. The rest of us know that's impossible—the LAPD can't even thin out traffic after a Dodger game.

Johnnie Cochran could sell you a plate of shit and have you asking for seconds. F. Lee Bailey's spewing out scenarios more deranged than a pitch meeting at the new Paramount Network. And Robert Shapiro's the only guy who uses a stretch limo to chase ambulances. And that demented little Tolkien character Carl Douglas should just shut the fuck up and go to a spa.

Of course, how could the case not be riveting with Judge Lance Ito at the helm? When Ito says "Jump," people say, "So, anyway I was . . ." I wish Ito would just cut the showbiz crap and just turn to O.J. and say, "So what's up with this shit, man, are you guilty or what?"

Even outside, the grounds around the courthouse look more like the souvenir gauntlet at the NASCAR championships. I'm fairly certain you can get a set of those "Free OJ" corn tongs and a "Guilty/Not Guilty" car freshener for under twenty bucks.

Finally, there's Orenthal James Simpson himself, sitting at the defense table, making more faces than Hugh Grant explaining things to Liz Hurley.

You know I honestly believe O.J. thinks he's innocent. I think he's strolling into the courtroom each day much the same way Ed Wood showed up on the set for *Plan 9 from Outer Space,* and he'll be utterly flabbergasted if the jury gives his little opus twelve thumbs down.

And yet, here's the really sad part—Instead of being repulsed by all this, every day, millions of us religiously tune in to rubberneck this intergalactic freak show.

The media claim that they're just doing their job, feeding the news appetite of the American people. I guess it's really not their fault that we happen to be bulimic.

The key thing we must all remember about the O.J. trial is that it is trial by flurry.

Lawyers on both sides bicker incessantly over matters that have precious little to do with discovering the truth. This thing is going slower than Jimmy Stewart reciting the *Mahabharata* on the back of an arthritic tortoise that's munching a quaalude on a humid Sunday afternoon in a hammock hung between two trees in the intensified gravity of the planet Jupiter.

And despite the fact that our belief in the American legal system has been stretched thinner than Robert Shapiro's conscience, we are simply going to have to wait for the cheap gears of justice to grind a decision out of this fake wood pepper mill. But I for one am through with it, and have been for a long while. He's guilty.

You know it, I know it, we all know it. So wait for sweeps week, schedule the jury's decision after "Seinfeld," announce that he's guilty, and throw away the fuckin' key. You're a punk, O.J. A bad guy. Go to hell.

Of course, that's just my opinion. I could be wrong.

what's
right
with
america

YOU KNOW, NORMALLY ON MY HBO SHOW I COME
out here week after week and piss on everything
like a drunk yard cat. You know that. That's my
job. I've always felt I'm paid to find things that are
wrong and then do my best to throw the switch on
the perimeter floods and light it up. Tonight we're
suppose to talk about what's *right* with America.
Now I know you've got to burrow pretty deep to
unearth any underlying confidence in a nation

that's sapped of its vigor, strafed by violence, and pummeled senseless by the debasement of every institution from the Armed Services to Baseball. That being said, *Are we gonna have some fun tonight?!* Yeah, all right. That was rhetorical. Now I don't want to get off on a rant here, but you know, there's a lot right with America! Nowadays, you just have to look a little harder for it. Sure, we're sick of paying for illegal immigrant kids to go to school and we're going to stop. But only a country that *did it* for a while can *stop* doing it. See? People don't ever consider that.

And okay, we nearly exterminated the Native Americans. Nobody tries to hide that anymore. But we *did* change our textbooks so the facts came out. I mean, who else does that? Only America. And as if admitting the truth wasn't enough, we don't even tax their casinos. And us—with a 4-trillion-dollar debt! I'm saying not taxing billions in Indian bingo loot is magnanimous and should be in the "What's Right with America" column!

How's about this—in America, we let people in prison read, study law, even work out so they can get themselves out of jail in much better mental and physical shape to resume their lives of crime. A lot of countries treat their criminals like animals, like sub-humans, as if they'd done something wrong! Not America. Not this great country.

I'm not a complete ethno-centrist. I went over to France earlier this year for a couple of months, to see if I might live there. And while I enjoyed my time in Paris, I should tell you that the French hate our guts. I cannot believe they actually gave us the Statue of Liberty. They must've been throwing it out anyway. Because these people detest us. They look at us and we are one, big, collective Jethro bearing down on them, rope belt and all. And you know something? In all fairness, we might be hicks, but at least we're hicks who tend to our armpits more frequently than once every time Comet Kohoutek is in the solar system. These people avoid showers like a blonde at the Bates Motel. They had to invent perfume. It wasn't an augmentation, it was a defense mechanism. Trust me, when Louis the XIV guillotined you, he was doing you a big favor separating your olfactory senses from your brainstem. "Yeah, Claude, paint the water lilies a little later. Right now I need you to pick up that loofa and storm the pit Bastille, all right?" Thank you, Pepe LePeux. I had a cabdriver over there, smelled like a man eating Gorgonzola cheese while getting a permanent inside the septic tank of a slaughterhouse. I said, "Hey, pal. There's an extra five in it for ya if you run over a fucking skunk." So, there's another reason why this country's great. We smell better than most.

Another reason we're great is because we create things here, things of unique beauty, things that unconsciously interweave the American attributes of ingenuity, optimism, gluttony, and narrow-mindedness. Things like: "All You Can Eat" Restaurants . . . The Clapper . . . Street-legal, semi-automatic grenade weapons that even the Tontons Macoute didn't have . . . The Temporary Insanity Plea . . . Cutting-edge CD-ROM technology used for porno . . . deep-fried cheese . . . bans on *toy* guns . . . rain ponchos for dogs . . Orange Julius . . . Orange County . . . beer can hats . . . plea bargaining . . . being able to plug your parents with bullets and getting acquitted . . indeed we're even free over here to subscribe to 500 channels of cable only to find out that that piece of shit, William Katt's superhero show, is on 498 of them . . . You know . . . As a matter of fact, you want to know what's right with America more than anything? Our right to speak out about everything that's *wrong* with it. And we're all free to vent at will—at least for the next couple of days till Gingrich takes over and straps the rat cage on our collective face.

You know . . . this really *is* a great country. Remind yourself of it once in a while. Take the family on Route 66, shop at the Galleria, buy a gun, have your breasts enlarged, have your penis lengthened, sue your neighbor, eat three Big Macs, drive 120 and pay the ticket, visit the White House—or better yet, jump the fence and go meet the Prez in person. He likes that. He really really likes that. *It's America, goddamn it!!*

Of course, that's just my opinion. I could be wrong.

teen

pregnancy

ISN'T IT IRONIC THAT SO MANY PEOPLE HAVE TO adopt children while teenagers who have no right being in the baby-making business are spewing out toddlers faster than a candy conveyor belt operated by Lucy Ricardo on methamphetamine?

A new survey in Wednesday's *USA Today* says that half of all teenagers have engaged in some sort of sexual activity. High school newspapers are now printing birth announcements. Our kids are having sex at younger and younger ages. Pretty soon, prophylactic companies will be selling condoms with a secret prize in every box. You know, when I was a kid, the closest I ever got to sex was getting a woody from holding my books on my lap during a bumpy school bus ride. Sure, there were always a couple of guys and a couple of girls in each class who were on the hormonal *Concorde*, but we treated their exploits like we treated NASA space shots—with respectful awe, yet a total ignorance of the physics involved. Nowadays, that has all changed. When it comes to reproduction, our country has become a giant all-night Kinko's.

Now I don't want to get off on a rant here, but the youth of America is screwing like there's no tomorrow, probably because to them it looks like there's no tomorrow.

Too often these days, a teenage girl's "inner child" is literally that. Our kids are having kids faster than Republicans can cut their school lunches. Our teen birthrate is twice that of England's, three times as high as Sweden's. It's the highest adolescent birthrate in the developed world. And it's spawned a generation of fatherless children who wind up joining gangs, or even worse, improv groups.

How did it come to pass that America's teenagers have gone from overcrowding phone booths to overcrowding the planet?

Well, a lot of these teenagers who are having kids themselves are doing so because they *want* to become pregnant, they *want* the attention, they *want* to feel loved. And that's a major tragedy right there. Parenting is the toughest job in the world. Ironically, it's the easiest job to get—you just have to screw up once and it's yours. Thirteen-year-olds having babies so that they can feel grownup. What happened to trying on Mom's heels and makeup? Christ, I still do that.

How do we begin to rectify this problem? Well, we can start by teaching sex education. A young boy shouldn't have to file forms under the Freedom of Information Act just to get the approximate shape and location of a girl's vagina. This type of useless mystery surrounding sex only adds to the desire.

And while we're at it, let's teach a follow-up class to sex education. Call it Reality 101—the *right* thing to do if you bring a bambino into this world. Hammering home to a sixteen-year-old teen that he or she is going to have to quit school, quit video games, quit "hangin' out," quit boogie-boardin',' and instead work a fifty-hour week dropping frozen chicken tenders into hot oil just so you can keep little "Scooter Junior" in Similac, well, trust me, that's a bigger deterrent to teenage sex than the backseat of a fuckin' Yugo.

Now, sure, some of these teens are so experienced they could be *teaching* sex education, but it's up to us to teach them the consequences of their postpubescent grope-fests.

It's sadly ironic that the breakdown of the nuclear family has actually resulted in the *increase* of family members. Wouldn't you rather go with your kid to a sex education class *now*, than a Lamaze class seven months from now?

And let me also speak to you semi-Joey Lawrence/Bobby Brown/Rico Suave wanna-bes out there—if you get a girl pregnant, marry her. I'm a firm believer in the "teenage shotgun wedding." *One* because it's the right thing to do, and *two*, because, hey, nowadays, most teenagers have shotguns anyway.

As for our esteemed leadership in Washington? Sometimes it would appear that these demagogues furtively crave teen pregnancies because they need the scape-goats.

Well, we need to get the Religious Right to take off their official Ralph Reed blinders and *wake up*. I know they'd rather have kids learn about sex the same way they did—from disgraced TV evangelists. But look, we all need mo-rality in our lives. But abstinence isn't working for *priests* these days, so I doubt it's going to work for teenagers cranked up on Nine Inch Nails and fruit coolers. So to all of you "Bu-Caynan-ites" out there—just calm down. No-body's passing out condoms to *increase* the sexual activity of kids. Condoms don't make babies—people do.

Listen, our kids have a void inside them—they're kids, for chrissakes—and if we don't fill that void with love, they'll fill the void with sex.

They're bombarded with imagery and attitudes every day that say it's okay to do just that. Let's stop making silicone boobs and pumped-up abs the only logo our kids ever see for "The Good Life." Then maybe we'll see a day when the only ovens our kids have buns in say "E-Z Bake" on the side. America, let's grow up about sex. Let's realize that a Surgeon General who speaks her mind about sex education, teen pregnancy, and preventative health care doesn't deserve to be Surgeon General . . . she deserves to be the fucking President of the United States.

Of course, that's just my opinion. I could be wrong.

the

presidency

Y'KNOW, BILL CLINTON CAN WALK SOLEMNLY
through the Rose Garden with Nelson Mandela
every day of the year and we'll still see a ruddy-
faced frat-rat who's probably wondering what the
presidential seal would look like on the ass of that
blond reporter in the second row.

Now I don't want to get off on a rant here, but
what has happened to the presidency?

The last half dozen presidents have been bunko artists who make Melvin Dumar look like he was Edward R. Murrow. Let's dust for prints. You had LBJ, the jug-eared sage of the South, whose Vietnam policy tore the country apart like a silk blouse marked down to $2.99 at a Target Assistant Manager's Day Sale.

You had Nixon: a fleshy homunculus with a paranoid psyche lodged in his whirring tin brain like a radioactive walnut. Nixon, with his preternatural sweaty brow and a beard so thick he had to shave while he was shaving.

And then there was Gerald Ford, whom I hold personally responsible for Chevy's talk show.

Enter Jimmy Carter, lusting in his heart and driving a VW Rabbit to the airport himself to pick up the Russian premier.

Which led us to Ronald Reagan, the aging spendthrift with the black enamel Bob's Big Boy hairdo who told the country that we *could* have our pie and eat it too. And we'd never get fat while we lay in bed, stupefied by potato chip grease and bourbon, a hand in our under-pants, watching "Lifestyles of the Rich and Famous," and hoping we wouldn't have to wait until *next* week to win the lottery.

And Reagan, Reagan begot Bush, the thin-lipped C student from Yale who spent more time out of the country than Roman Polanski. George Bush, a President who looked all the more like a king for the fool he kept with him—the freckle-faced muffin head from the great state of Indiana, Dan Quayle

And it tells me a lot about how far the presidency has fallen that a guy like Quayle can actually throw his jughead crown into the ring, in public, in print, and not be hounded from the room in a hail of desk staplers, dictionaries, small trash barrels, and half-eaten boxes of vegetable fried rice. I am appalled that this Chuzzlewit can actually aspire to the presidency outside the walls of a mental institution and people don't tie him down and scrape his frontal lobes with a trowel like some demented *Clockwork Orange* Droogie who's due to be rewired.

No, our expectations have shriveled to the point where people just nod and write him a check. "Yeah, okay. President Quayle. Beautiful. Where's the bathtub with the Kool-Aid?"

And that dumps us out at the Clinton presidency—Faust meets L'il Abner. Bill Clinton . . . Cute kid, but I'm not exactly getting the "Ghandi-ji" vibe off him at this point. Not a bad man, but not a good man either. Not a man of character, solid and sure, principled and even-handed, but an average Joe, tugged all around the game board of life by his need to be liked, his desire to press his flesh against the flesh of pretty girls, his love of fatty foods, rail drinks, and sappy Fleetwood Mac songs, peddling gimcrack philosophies to a simple beat any clunk can dance to.

Sure, Bill has a few good ideas, and he seems to genuinely want what's best for the country, but so what? Does that make him a President of consequence like Jefferson, Lincoln, or Truman? No, it doesn't. He's only the President because every four years, we have to pick one. That's all. He took a ticket, waited awhile, got his order, and pretty soon he'll leave the restaurant. We'll clean his table and get ready for the next shmo with aspirations beyond his capabilities.

Well, I'll be honest with you, folks, what I'm looking for is somebody to just swipe the table clean in a frustrated *Five Easy Pieces* rage because the service in this place is really starting to suck. I mean what happened? What do we see these days when we look at a President? A schemer, a poll-taking self-aggrandizer who knows how—when he is caught red-handed cheating on his taxes, humping a campaign volunteer, or squelching the common good for PAC contributions—to run down to Kmart and wade into a bunch of hamburger-addler wage slaves, snatch up one of their wally-eyed babies stunned into placidity by mother's milk mixed liberally with diet Coke and Nuprin, kiss it for the cameras, then zip back to the Oval Office while the photo-op is developed and mainlined into the homes of good folks who will see a man who's done wrong, surely, but loves babies. And that's America: dulled by mindless entertainment to the hard facts, and hopeful that the Big Lie is really the big truth.

Well, the Big Lie just isn't going to work anymore. And I think that if this President and future Presidents really want to be taken to the bosom of the American people, they're gonna have to come clean with us. They're going to have to drop the obfuscation, drop the smoke and mirrors, and the pretense and denial, drop the weapons-grade bullshit, look America squarely in the eye and say, "Yeah, I inhaled it. Then I drank the fuckin' bong water."

Of course, that's just my opinion. I could be wrong.

what

men

want

from

women

CHRIST, MOST MEN DON'T EVEN KNOW WHAT
they want from Ben & Jerry's much less from
women.

Now I don't want to get off on a rant here, but
what do *I* want from a woman? Well, nothing. I
personally am happily married to a beautiful, sexy,
intelligent woman, and therefore am completely
satisfied physically, emotionally, and spiritually.

But I do remember what it was like to be one of you, one of the walking dead staggering from seedy singles bar to seedy singles bar using your unrequited, and might I add diminutive, excuse for a hard-on as a sexual divining rod in a pathetic, fruitless effort to find a woman, or at least somebody who has a few of the body parts, who might actually fake nominal interest in that dog-eared, hackneyed, nightmarish story that you have the nerve to call your life.

So I can sympathize.

But I can't really speak for the entire male collective, which is so diverse it makes the bar scene in *Star Wars* look like an IBM management seminar.

I will say that one constant theme in man's interaction with women is the Madonna/whore complex, and believe me that's just the tip of the Oedipal iceberg. Quite frankly, I think when you get a guy alone he'll readily confess he not only has a Madonna/whore complex, he's got a Mother, Au Pair, Catholic Nun, Hullabaloo Dancer, Julie Newmar–Cat Woman, Asian Cigarette girl, Pamela Anderson in a Plexiglas House, Miss Hathaway with a Riding Crop–complex. And you should also understand this about men. Men aren't designed to be introspective. We don't always know how we're feeling. We don't even know how we're feeling. Your vagina goes inward, you introspect. Our penises point outward—we want to knock things over with it, all right.

I know the myth is that men want—Traci Lords in the bedroom, Julia Child in the kitchen, Hazel around the house, Lesley Visser during a game, Mary Poppins for the children, Cha Cha Muldowney in traffic, Dr. Quinn medicine chick when we're sick, Mary Richards at work, Mother Teresa when we come home with leprosy, Gertrude Stein in conversation, the body of Sophia Loren in *Boy on a Dolphin* combined with the voice of Sade, and to top it all off the IQ of Anna Nicole Smith, because, of course, we don't want to feel too threatened.

So, that's the myth of what we want, what's the reality? Well, first off put that *Cosmo* article down right now and back slowly away from the magazine!

Now go to the window and take a deep breath. You must clear your head of bullshit articles like "How to Trick Your Man into Cooking Tex-Mex." Trick me? How's about *asking* me? And then I'll be able to tell you I don't have a fucking clue what Tex-Mex is, okay?!

But what I look for in a woman is what most guys look for in a woman, and what most women look for in a guy: somebody I want to be with. Somebody who's fun, intelligent, attractive. Somebody it won't be hard to spend time with. All that other stuff is just details.

What else do men want? How about being treated like a lady once in a while?

All right, I'm not supposed to do this. I'm not supposed to reveal the master list to all you non tri-pods, but what the hell. Here goes. Here's what men want from women. One through ten:

ONE—We want you to understand that we don't give a shit about clothes. All right. Yours or ours. All we need is one pair of tennies and one pair of church shoes. That's it.

TWO—Don't talk to us while the television is on. All right. Very simple. Television is off, we talk. Television is on, we don't talk.

THREE—When you're behind the wheel of a car, if you want to get aggressive, that's fine, but don't give somebody the finger and expect me to defend your honor when Steroid Lad comes over swinging a pair of nun-chucks, all right?

FOUR—Would it kill you to watch *The Godfather* with me for the fifty-seventh time?

FIVE—Hey, I'm sorry, but some of us see a beautiful sunset and think, "You know I'll betcha my accountant is boning me up the ass."

SIX—You go see *Nell* by yourself, all right? I met enough chicks like that at Helena's when I was single.

SEVEN—Have a sense of humor. Without a sense of humor a relationship lasts about as long as William Burroughs in the Boston Marathon.

EIGHT—Work out your job-related anger before we have sex. Just because Helmut, the office boy, brought you the *cup* of lima bean consommé instead of the *bowl* of lima bean consommé from Soup Plantation, I don't want to end up in the friction burn groin ward at Cedars-Sinai. All right?

NINE—Don't ask us to cry. As much as you say you want us to cry, you don't really want us to cry. You hate it when we cry. I've tried crying in front of my wife. She enjoyed it for about thirty seconds and then started thinking, "Why in the fuck did I marry this hamster?"

AND TEN, be patient. Hold us. Love us unconditionally. Help us out of this testosterone-induced fog we dwell in and lead us into the light. Or if that's asking too much, how's about a big sloppy blow job once in a while.

Of course, that's just my opinion. I could be wrong.

exercise

YOU KNOW, BILL CLINTON IS LIVING PROOF THAT
physical exercise can be a complete waste of time,
isn't he? I mean the more he jogs, the bigger he
gets. You realize that if this guy is reelected, the
leader of the free world will be Bib the Michelin
Man.

Thank you. Did we go Pavlov there with the sign?!
Not that I'm one to talk. The other day, I noticed

my wife had hung a picture on the wall of her with another man.

A man whose chin and cheekbones had definition, a man who didn't need to suck in his gut like Hasselhoff in a public sauna just to get through the monologue on his own highly acclaimed HBO show. And as I continued to gaze at the photo I realized the svelte stranger was in fact me. I used to be in shape. What the hell happened?

Well, what happened to me has happened to a lot of us. One night you and your wife finish off a large sausage pizza with extra sausage, and you notice she didn't have any. You think uhh, you think, "Boy, I should work this meal off," then you lay down on the couch for a little fifteen-*year* nap.

Now I don't want to get off on a rant here, but what is it with America's "Can't fit into my Calvin Klein's Like Obsession" with fitness? Isn't our slow but sure descent into a Hitchcockian silhouette just evolution in its purest form? And quite frankly, isn't all this fitness crap a feeble attempt to defy Darwin's relentless glacier? In short, isn't our species meant to look like Fat Albert?

When I think about it, the only exercise program that has ever worked for me is occasionally getting up in the morning and jogging my memory to remind myself exactly how much I hate to exercise.

Running? I keep hearing about this "runner's high," but I must have gotten ahold of some bad shit, because I uhh I tried it once, and six blocks in, I was on all fours vomiting in the gutter like George Bush at a Benihana.

Walking? Walking? If it's so good for you, how come my mailman looks like Jabba the Hut with a quirky thyroid?

The treadmill? You take your eyes off the thing for one second and you end up like Gary Busey on . . . well, let's say, any weekend. You know, my wife doesn't mind my running on the treadmill but she gets a little miffed when I squeal at her to refill my hanging water bottle while I pee in the wood shavings that I've spread out on the floor. Then there's the StairMaster. As in walking up the stairs for a half an hour. If I want to do that I'll move back to my first shit-hole apartment in New York.

Aerobics? The only reason I like watching "Sweatin' to the Oldies" is because Richard Simmons is working his ass off and he's still not in any better shape than me. Hey, Richard, if I need low impact aerobics, I'll masturbate, all right? If I need high impact, I'll masturbate again.

Or of course you can take the ultimate easy way out—steroids. With steroids, you just keep getting older and older and bigger and bigger until you eventually have to retire to a game preserve and have kids throw pennies at your snout.

Hellooo, guys, the crotchal irony is that steroids only make one thing smaller and get this—it's your penis. And if you remember correctly, the paucity of a dick in your life is what got you into steroids in the first place, okay?

And as for private health clubs, they are just getting too damn complicated. You know, there's nothing quite as humiliating as finishing a thirty-minute workout on a piece of gym equipment only to have the instructor tell you you've been sitting on it backward.

And while we're at it, someone explain to me why anyone would want to go to a place called a "family" fitness center?

Why should your family burn off their pent-up energies at a gym when you can all accomplish the same thing for free at home with a series of ugly, confrontational shouting matches?

And then there's the stretch class at the health club. My wife suggested we take a stretch class. And I said, don't expect me to do any of that Jean-Claude Van Damme kitchen counter shit. My groin muscles are as intractable as Wayne La Pierre at the NRA's annual Skeetapalooza Show.

Hey, I have only one fitness goal. Like most of you, I'd like to be able to run a few down and outs with my sons at the family picnic without having to dial up Randy

Mantooth and the boys to sprint over carrying an IV with ringers.

I think any aspirations beyond that can be placed under the heading of narcissistic overkill. Folks, the bottom line is this—the last animals that let their heads get really small while their bodies got really big . . . ended up in our gas tanks, okay? So the next time you look in the mirror and see more pork than a congressional subcommittee, do something about it. Go to the garage, pick up your old dumbbells, walk back inside the house, and smash the fuck out of that mirror.

Of course, that's just my opinion. I could be wrong.

marriage

A SURVEY OUT THIS WEEK CLAIMS THE AVERAGE
married couple has sex on average only twice a
month. Guys, I guess that's the reason they call it
"tying the knot."

You know, when I hear the phrase "wedding ceremony," I think of a big church service, a huge
three-tiered cake, and elated friends and family
throwing rice at the happy newlyweds.

But nowadays the reality of the wedding has become pre-nuptial agreements longer than transcripts of the O.J. trial, lesbian rabbis with pierced eyebrows performing the ceremony, and wedding vows written by the bride and groom that are so sickeningly schmaltzy they make *The Bridges of Madison County* look like Milton's *Paradise Lost.*

But the changes in the wedding ceremony are superficial and harmless when compared to the deeper underlying changes taking place in the institution of marriage itself.

Now I don't want to get off on a rant here, but the institution of marriage is coming undone faster than Liza Minnelli on a Barbara Walters special. Couples are breaking up like a four-thousand-year-old Peruvian vase shipped UPS. And that's too bad, because I think marriage can be one of the most rewarding experiences you will have on this planet—*if* you meet the right person.

If you don't, I'll bet you it can be as tedious, ugly, and soul-crushing as driving on the 5 Freeway to Knott's Berry Farm with the windows up and no air-conditioning on Labor Day weekend with Kathie Lee and Regis in the car after they've had bean burritos for lunch. Sorry, Kathie Lee, but it's getting too thick lately, don't you think?

Hell, the vows are scary enough. I mean, "We are gathered here to witness the *joining* of two people . . ." Joining. Could we come up with a slightly more industrial term, huh? How about, "soldering"? Yeah, have a couple of guys from the machinists' union swing by, drop the welder's masks, and handle this part of the ceremony. You know, it seems like the only two times they pronounce you anything in life is when they pronounce you "man and wife" or "dead on arrival."

Just elope. Spare yourselves the sadistic ritual known as "the wedding plans," where, guys, quite frankly, your opinion is about as important as the foreword in a Jackie Collins novel.

Now, I personally am a very lucky man. My wife Ali is a wonderful, intelligent, beautiful, sexy, funny woman whom I adore, and she returns the favor. As a matter of fact, my wife walks on the ground I worship. I continue to feel deeply passionate toward her. In fact, the other night I was making love to my wife and she said, "Deeper . . . deeper . . ." So I started whispering Nietzsche quotes into her ear. "Man is a rope stretched over the abyss . . ." She said, "Whoa. Not that fuckin' deep. I'm trying to get off over here."

Incidentally, Nietzsche, of course, for the uninitiated is number sixty-six for the Green Bay Packers. Incidentally, if and when your mate ever asks you about your sexual history when you were single, it's best to bear in mind Jack Nicholson's line from *A Few Good Men*—"You want to know the truth? You can't handle the truth!"

After seven years of marriage, I'm sure of two things—
first, never wallpaper together, and second, you'll need
two bathrooms . . . both for her. The rest is a mystery,
but a mystery I love to be involved in. You know what's
disheartening? A lot of men don't want to get married.
They say things like, "I don't want to compromise." Oh
yeah, like you're not compromising now. Living alone,
holes in your undies, jacking off to "The Price is Right"
models so many times your hand is translucent.

Yeah. Why would *you* ever want to compromise, Mr.
Cimino?

The rule is simple for marriage. It's the journey, not the
destination that makes it work. Now I know a lot of us
are the product of a union so Gothic in its dysfunction it
makes the couples in *Who's Afraid of Virginia Woolf* look
like Steve and Eydie. But we cannot let that deter us.

Sure, marriage is scary. It's like sky diving—you can prac-
tice all you want on the ground but it's not until you
jump from ten thousand feet that you'll know if you're
fucked or not.

That's why I have a special marriage proposal for you—a
bill to create a mandatory waiting period for marriage li-
censes.

Like buying firearms, marriage is a highly volatile situation
with potentially tragic results. We've already got the Brady

Bill, which mandates a waiting period for buying a gun—
it's time to have a waiting period for getting married and
starting a family. We could call it the Brady *Bunch* Bill.
Because remember—marriages don't destroy relationships,
people do.

Of course, that's just my opinion. I'm not married to it.

equality

of

the

sexes

NOW I DON'T WANT TO GET OFF ON A RANT HERE, but we trivialize women's issues in this country by fixating on the insignificant and ignoring the consequential. It's unbelievable to me. With all the serious inequities heaped on womanhood: the fact that they don't get paid equally; the fact that they're often brutalized by incomplete male monsters. What do we focus on? We focus on the bullshit, the freak show, the pubic hair on the Coke.

The warnings from the strident feminist groups about anything male including telling women to beware of the
Heimlich come-on. All this sort of bullshit.

And then we worry about the New England Patriots
locker room situation—this is Lindbergh-like headlines in
this country, for months. Some female reporter goes into
the locker room, a couple of second-stringers dangle their
Johnsons in front of her. She's so freaked out now she's
got to move out of the country.

There's that Margaret Bourke-White spirit for ya, huh?

Evidently she's in some "I brushed up against it" clinic in
Lugano, Switzerland. But you know something? Let me
advance the radical theory that she shouldn't have been in
the locker room. And the reason she shouldn't have been
in the locker room is because she shouldn't have wanted
to be in the locker room. Women in this country will
make their greatest strides when they begin to realize that
there are certain bullshit male rituals that they shouldn't
want to have a fuckin' thing to do with.

Don't you see? You're better than that! You're 52 percent
of the electorate for Christ's sake . . . take the reins, we
fucked up, we can't do it. Don't you see the cosmic tip-
off? You are the life givers, you must be the ones who
save us. Aim your sights a little higher and go for the big
piñata. Fuck the locker room, vote the Arlen Specters out
of office. I don't want to turn this into Susan Faludi's deb

ball . . . but if you really want to break the back of the male domination in this country, get together and collectively cut us off.

Because you see . . . you love to fuck, but we need to fuck, all right? And you should just get together and deny us sex en masse. The great American Poke Out. I guarantee you within two weeks you rule the country. If you thought Renfield was blindly allegient to Dracula, we will be the Stepford penises.

And you know, you can start by taking back control of your bodies. And I hope you all saw the flare go off two weeks ago, it finally happened . . . someone in the right to life movement killed a doctor. To really point out the heinous nature of this crime let's use their terminology . . . The right to life movement aborted a child . . . in the two-hundredth trimester.

Now I don't believe in abortion, but more importantly, I don't believe in the right to a life without any rights. And I think that some of the people in the right to life movement should get a fucking life before they begin to tell other people what to do with theirs.

Of course, that's just my opinion. I could be wrong.

air

travel

NOW I DON'T WANT TO GET OFF ON A RANT HERE,
but flying in this country has turned into an amazingly arduous process, especially boarding the plane, which has now become this tedious Bataan death march with American Tourister overnight bags. I get stuck behind this one guy, who takes forever to get situated. He's clogging the aisle like a piece of human cholesterol jammed in the pas-

sengerial artery. You just want to get that soft drink cart and flush his ass out the back door. He's folding that sport jacket like he's in the color guard at Arlington National Cemetery.

Or else I get stuck behind a wizard who wants to beat the system by gaffer-taping a twine handle onto a refrigerator-freezer box and calling it "carry on." Wedging it into the overhead with hydraulic jacks. It's like trying to get Pavarotti into a wet suit, for Christ's sake.

And exactly when did stewardesses in this country get so fucking cranky? I know it's a tough job. There's got to be a thousand different ways to tie that neckerchief but why piss on me, huh? You know the worst thing about it is they don't even come clean with you and tell you how much they hate you. They treat you with that highly contrived air of mock civility, that tight, pursed-lip grin where they nod agreement with everything you say. You know right behind that face plate they barely tolerate your very existence. I'd rather they just come out in the open and say, "Hey, listen, asshole. When I was eighteen years old, I made a horrible vocational error, all right? I turned my entire adult life in for cheap airfare to Barbados. Now I've got hair with the tensile strength of Elsa Lanchester in *Bride of Frankenstein*. I haven't met Mr. Right. I'm a waitress in a bad restaurant at thirty thousand feet. Jam your Diet Slice up your ass, all right?" At least show me something. Come down the aisle like the old broad in *From*

Russia with Love with the knife point coming out of her shoe. "Peanuts, Mr. Bond?"

What about when you leave the plane and they've got them propped by the front door in that complete android catatonic stupor where they look like the Yul Brynner robot from *Westworld* when he blew a headpipe and iced Marcus Welby's assistant. "Bye. Bye. Bye. Bye." It's like your stockbroker on Thorazine or something.

And am I the only one who likes to get on a plane and unwind with a good book? Sit there in a little peace and quiet. I'm constantly in conversation with complete strangers—always being approached by these overly ebullient Jonathan Livingston Human types. This eighteen-year-old kid who's on his way back from Aruba and wants to show me this skull bong he purchased there that's carved out of volcanic rock. You know he's always got a dream he wants me to interpret for him. What am I, Queequeg? And you're afraid to not talk to him. You never know who the fucking terrorist is on the plane. I'd hate to alienate anybody who's looking for a prom date to Valhalla.

There's a lot of terrorism in the air, but you know when you walk through the air terminal and see the crack security people manning the perimeter, I think we all sleep the sleep of angels. Came into Phoenix the other day, the woman working the X-ray machine had the attention span of Boo Radley. She's sitting there like Captain Pike from "Star Trek." She had a channel flicker. She's watching baggage from other airports, for Christ's sake.

You think pilots make fun of those guys who bring them the last ten feet into the terminal with those cone flashlights? "Well, thank you, Vasco da Gama. I kited in from Malaysia, you're going to take me the last furlong, Captain Eveready. I hope you don't blow a D-cell. I'd hate to be stuck out here in the Bermuda Tarmac for the rest of my life."

What about those masks that drop down in the event of decompression? That's a pretty flimsy-looking apparatus, isn't it? Doesn't this look remarkably like a Parkay margarine cup on the end of an enema bag or something? They always have these bizarre instructions to start the flow of oxygen. "Tug down lightly on the cord." Yeah, you know when I'm shoulder-rolling at seven hundred miles per hour, "lightly" just isn't in my fucking vocabulary, all right? You know people are going to be Conaning those things right off the bulkhead. Something intrinsically cruel having the last forty seconds of your life turn into a "Lucy" skit.

I think instead of oxygen, they ought to pump in nitrous oxide. This way, if the plane does wreck—that first rescue team comes onto the scene—you're up in a tree still strapped in your seat just laughing your ass off. Guys say,

"Bobby, get over here. Look how hip this guy is. I mean, he's naked, he's blue, he's howling. This cat is centered, huh?"

You know what I hate is when you're sitting in coach class and they pull that curtain on first class. Oh, I see, they paid an extra forty dollars and I'm a fucking leper. I always get the feeling that if the plane's about to wreck, the front compartment breaks off into a little Goldfinger mini-plane. They're on their way to Rio and I'm a charcoal briquet on the ground.

You know who I feel sorry for in the whole air-travel scenario? It's the poor bastard who has to drive the jetway. You know that little accordion tentacle that weaves its way out to meet the plane? Everybody else is Waldo Pepperin' around in their Bobby Lansing leather bomber jackets, the right stuff coursing through their veins as they push the outside of the envelope. Your job is to drive the building.

A lot of qualifications to sit next to that exit door, huh? When did that happen? I've been a physical klutz for years. I'm like Clouseau. Nobody's ever said a word. All of a sudden they want me to be a fucking Navy SEAL. I guess they want to be sure the person sitting there doesn't panic in the event that the plane goes down in water. Item number 8 on the qualification list was "You must not be Ted Kennedy."

Of course, that's just my opinion. I could be wrong.

america

the

touchy

NOW I DON'T WANT TO GET OFF ON A RANT HERE, but that's the problem with America. You can't tease anybody. I read now that gay people don't even want to be called gay anymore. They now wish to be referred to as Asian.

"Hey, what's Dennis saying there, man? Is Dennis saying all Asians are gay? Is Dennis saying all gays are Asian?" You know what I'm saying . . . all Asians are gay.

Now somewhere out there, there's an Asian person taking pen to paper in protest. And I want you to hear me out . . . put the pen down, it was a joke. Walk away from it. Let it go. It never happened. It was a comment on how pathetically neurotic we've all become over our own little piece of turf. Obviously, you know I don't believe that all Asians are gay. For Christ's sake there's a billion of you, I know somebody's fucking out there, okay?

And yet this is what it's come to. This is what it's come to in contemporary America. Everybody's broken off into these petulant little Travis Bickle tribes. Everybody walks the perimeter of their own damaged esteem ever-vigilant against an incursion by They, Them. The Other Guys. Everybody's touchy and everybody's encouraged to be touchy, everybody that is . . . except me: the White Anglo-Saxon male. I'm everybody's asshole. Black people think I'm oppressive and physically deficient. Women think I'm oafish and horny. Gay people think I'm overly macho and latently homosexual. And Asians think I'm lazy and stupid. Hey, you think you've got an ax to grind? I'm fuckin' Paul Bunyan over here, okay, folks?

And if I'm expected to be genial, there's a principle of reciprocity here, I expect you to do the same. Why are we so hung up on the name calling? We are all such overgrown babies. As it turns out adult life is just tall grade school: "You suck," "With your mouth," "Hi, my mouth," "Hi, me." It's embarrassing. I can't believe it, the playground is way back there in the mist We've got to let it go and get on with it. Why do you think we get hung up on all the little bullshit?

I have a theory: I think we're far less evolved ourselves. I know we consider ourselves to be very nineties creatures, we take it all in, we deal with it . . . we put it back out. We are just the hippest little creatures, but you know something? I think in a deep gut level we're scared shitless. We live in a madhouse and it's brought into our living rooms on a day-to-day level via CNN. And we see things that we probably aren't equipped to even vaguely get our head around. Children in Somalia . . . the atrocities in Bosnia—Cal-a-frag-a-listic-ex-pee-al-a-docious. I think all this shit comes down and we think, "Christ, it really is out of control."

So what we do is we take all the little bullshit things, we trump it up into something bigger than it actually is, something we can mold and handle, and in some vague pathetic way keep our feet tethered to the planet.

And that's why this entire country has turned into Gladys Kravitz from "Bewitched."

Of course, that's just my opinion. I could be wrong.

james

stockdale

3/17/93

NOW I DON'T WANT TO GET OFF ON A RANT HERE,
but the public crucifixion of James Stockdale
is one of my lowest moments as an American
citizen.

Now I know he's become a buzzword in this culture for doddering old man, but let's look at the
record, folks. This guy was the first guy in and the
last guy out of Vietnam, a war that many Ameri-

cans, including our present President, did not want to dirty their hands with. The reason he had to turn his hearing aid on at that debate is because those fucking animals knocked his eardrums out when he wouldn't spill his guts. He teaches philosophy at Stanford University, he's a brilliant, sensitive, courageous man. And yet he committed the one unpardonable sin in our culture: he was bad on television.

Somewhere out there Paddy Chayefsky must be laughing his ass off. We should be ashamed of ourselves. Could he have been our Vice President? Of course he could've been our Vice President. You think Al Gore is a charismatic visionary? His favorite film is *Tron,* for Christ's sake.

And how tough can this job be, look who did it for the last four years. Dan Quayle's head is emptier than a Jack in the Box in downtown Seattle. He shouldn't have been second in command of the Hekawi Indians from "F Troop," much less the third most powerful nation on the face of this planet. Always had that freshly tasered Norma Desmond look on his face. His eyes are glazed over like Ban Roll-On applicators. And you know, this is not to say that I won't miss Dan Quayle. Because to me he was the Rosetta Stone of contemporary American comedy. But let's face facts, he deserved the vice presidency like Elvis deserved his black belt, all right? I always thought of this guy as like Dan Tanna's assistant, Binzer, on the old "Vegas" show. You let him answer the phone but he does not drive the T-bird.

And you know something, I'll bet you any money he's thinking of running for President five years from now. The day Dan Quayle's our President is the day Shelley Winters runs with the bulls at Pamplona.

Of course, that's just my opinion. I could be wrong.

the

gop

first

hundred

days

4/7/95

WOW, IT CERTAINLY HAS BEEN AN EVENTFUL
hundred days for the Republicans, huh? Since
Gingrich and the Republicans have assumed control of Congress, all of us have remained glued to
our televisions. We are awestruck by the speed at
which all this is taking place—the never-ending
sessions, the incessant bickering, the controversy
surrounding the reliability of DNA testing . . .
Wait a second. That's another freak show.

Now I don't want to get off on a rant here, but I can't believe all of the incredible changes that have swept across this great nation of ours in the Republicans' first hundred days:

The deficit now stands at zero; homelessness and poverty have, like polio, been eradicated forever; and violent crime and illiteracy are things of the past. All hallucinating aside, maybe, just maybe, we should actually think about giving the Republicans a little breathing room. After all, it's only been a measly one hundred days and that's roughly the length of the new cast introductions on "Saturday Night Live."

And I guess you've got to hand it to old Newt and the boys. They have actually accomplished some of what they set out to do—line item veto, common sense legal reform, trimming government waste.

Good for them! In a city where men keep more women than they do promises, give Gingrich his due: He has followed through on his swing to the pragmatic right.

On the negative side of the ledger, the GOP, which has long railed against the evils of career politicians, promised that within the first hundred days, they would impose term limits on members of Congress. But last week, House Republicans voted squarely against public opinion and rejected term limits. You know, I'll bet when it comes to legislating term limits on benefits to unwed single mothers and welfare recipients, my guess is they'll pass that like a burrito dipped in Vaseline. I guess some things will never change.

Elected office still contains more perks than Elvis Presley's nightstand.

Another negative as I see it is that the new balanced budget amendment has more harsh cuts in it than a Clive Barker film edited for airline use—heavy-handed cuts—heavy-handed cuts that remind you the Republican way of solving problems is like shooting at the rats in your rowboat with your .45.

But as far as I'm concerned, the "Contract with America" really metamorphs into a throw rug for your parakeet's cage when they start screwing around with the school lunch program.

Newt wants to eliminate federal responsibility for free breakfasts in public schools and turn it over to the states. Hey, folks, the states can't pave fucking roads! And besides, you think Newt really knows firsthand what it's like to miss a meal? Huh? There are pelicans envious of this guy's gullet. Gingrich has more chins than an "impeach Al D'Amato rally." Yeah. You gotta quit moaning or I am gonna turn on you viciously. Either laugh or don't but don't give me that whiny moan shit all night.

Yeah, mess with the school lunch program. We don't have enough violence in school, let's add hunger into the equation. Then the kids will have to bring Gloch nine-millimeter handguns to school, because, you see, they won't be gang-bangers anymore, they'll be hunter-gatherers.

Okay, those are some of the specifics of the contract I quibble with. But even more disturbing is this stubborn, retro-minded urge by the Republicans to return to the so-called good old days. Listen, I'm somewhat sympathetic. Quite frankly, I understand the Republican frustration with modern life in general. But the difference between the Republicans and me is that I am ultimately capable of being jolted back to reality. They don't want to come back. They want it to be the 1950s really badly.

Unfortunately, they refuse to acknowledge one pertinent fact: the fifties sucked, all right! Just ask women, African Americans, anybody who was blacklisted, and the Big Bopper.

So what I'm saying is, as much as the Republicans long for the salad days of Roy Cohn, we will never achieve that gold-plated era again. Because, we're here now. Can't we set the wayback machine ahead a little, Shermie?

Now, as frustrating as that inability to return to simpler times may be to you Republicans, you—as politicians— cannot let that frustration turn into ugly anger. You leave that to me. Because no matter how rancorous I get, no matter how many big words I come perilously close to misusing, no matter how many profanities I stack up like dirty dishes at Brando's place, nothing I do will result in the school lunch program being trifled with.

Nothing I do will result in billionaire asbestos magnates living tax free on yachts a half-inch off the Florida coast.

Nothing I do will yank a family out of their home and into a refrigerator box on the all-too-mean streets.

And so, in response to the Contract with America, I propose my Contract with the Republicans: You do your job—create legislation to help Americans become not only more responsible, but also more compassionate, more tolerant, and more caring, and dare I say it, even more loving, and in exchange, you leave the bitter, callous, caustic, searing, vituperative, bile-filled, venomous, blistering, I can't believe Sonny Bono is actually one of my fucking leaders, bitchfest . . . you, uh, leave that to responsible pros like me.

Of course, that's just my opinion. I could be wrong.

pro

sports

strikes

12/23/94

WE GOT NO BASEBALL. WE GOT NO HOCKEY. IF IT weren't for my rotisserie cockfight league I would have never gotten through the year. And I should say up front that I have a lot more trouble with the baseball strike than I do the hockey lockout. Hockey players seem to bust their ass, give you good return on your dollar, and quite frankly, it looks like the new commissioner, Gary Bettman, he seems to be somewhat of a Napoleonic creep. So I think I'm on the players' side there.

But let's be honest—these labor disputes aren't about the need for salary caps or free agency. The real reason is deeper than that, and it's symptomatic of what's wrong everywhere in America, from our out-of-control legal system to our out-of-control health care system, to our out-of-control governmental system. Pure and simple: we're talking greed here. It's a never-ending quest for the biggest and best grail.

Now I don't want to get off on a rant here, but how can Americans still cherish baseball, a sport whose owners, given the chance, would place a Coors logo on home plate, and whose heroes, given the chance, would charge seven-year-old fans fifty bucks for a mug of day-old tobacco chew? We should stop deluding ourselves: Professional baseball in America is no longer a collection of Norman Rockwell tableaux of umpires feeling for rain or corn-fed outfielders standing in green fields of honor.

Baseball is what it is: just another profession, no more, no less.

I think baseball should recognize the fact that we had no World Series this year and yet nobody protested in the streets, nobody got in the Kool-Aid line, nobody even blinked, for chrissakes. What the players and owners of all major league sports have to remember is that people have this innate ability to switch from one form of entertainment to another. Just ask the guys that banked on vaudeville or bought stock in Betamax, or better yet, ask Gary Burghoff and McLean Stevenson . . . they're sharing a pad, aren't they?

I sometimes think back to the days when I could rely on professional sports as a video soporific. It seemed like a perfect scheme—baseball took you to football, football took you to basketball and hockey, basketball and hockey took you back to baseball again, with a few days off to get your teeth cleaned. We had it set up so only a few professional athletes actually had to spend their lives doing something. The rest of us could just sit back and watch. It was fucking beautiful. A whole nation of unshaven men sitting in their tattered undies on plaid couches, expanding like doughnuts on a jelly injector, watching a bunch of assholes play games. But the assholes who play the games couldn't get enough from the assholes who own the teams, and so the rest of us have been forced to confront the fact that we were the biggest assholes of all for being so fascinated by it.

So you know what's happened? We've actually been forced to participate in our own lives. And you know what? It turns out, it's more fun to play baseball than it is to watch it. It's more fun to get out with my friends, my kids, my wife, and do something on the weekend than it is to watch a couple of jag-offs punch each other on skates.

Hey, you know, I've wasted too much time and put on too much weight watching other people play games. Don't bother settling the strikes, we don't want you back. You've ruined the illusion that any of it matters. What matters now is my life, my family. And the fact that Christmas is the day after tomorrow. And here's a little jingle for you boys—

(Sung to "Deck the Halls")

Deck the halls with balls of holly
All the other balls are locked away

'Tis the season for sheer folly
Everybody wants a raise in pay

Sleazy owners, cheesy players
From New York, all the way, to L.A.

All of them are greedy bastards
They can go to hell, we'll pay their way!

Of course, that's just my opinion. I could be wrong.

homosexuality

NOW I DON'T WANT TO GET OFF ON A RANT HERE,
but I need to have a little tête-à-tête with my heterosexual brothers and sisters. Could we get over
this gay thing, please, like, like now? Gay men and
women have been around since the dawn of time,
which predates even Jesse Helms by twenty years.
"Why do they do it? Where does it come from? Is
it environmental or genetic?" Hey, I don't care if
they find a chiffon scarf on the X chromosome—

190

the important thing is, homosexuality is here to stay. So
many people are into so many different things sexually,
why single out a group of people and hound them, beat
them, decry their existence, deprive them of jobs even
in the military—the one place every unemployable American knows he can go for a plate of beans and a dental
plan.

Who cares about homosexuality, really? I mean who cares
what coupling gives any consenting adult pleasure? All we
should care about is that people are going home and getting off, somehow, with someone, anyone. Because a person who gets off tends not to be a nut who gets off offing
people.

About the only people I might quibble with are bisexuals,
because I think we all agree at some point that these
people are just incredibly greedy motherfuckers. I don't
ask much from a human being, but come down off the
fence and pick a hole. All right. I don't care what you
fuck, but fuck it regularly.

Now this is not to say I don't have my differences with
some members of the gay community. When I'm watching
the Gay Pride parade, and the "Genitals Are Our Friends"
float cruises by, with two leather-bound Eraserheads
dressed up as Timmy and Tommy, the Testicle Twins,
sure, I get the same creepy feeling I get when I hear
Shatner sing. But the bottom line is, that's their business
at the end of the day, it's relatively harmless business.

That being said—that we need to be tolerant of the sexual proclivities of others—there are those who fall outside the great campfire of heterosexual weenie-roasts and schwing-a-longs and they have got to stop them from wasting their time looking for across-the-board validation. It's just not gonna happen. Not on this planet—not in our lifetime.

ACT UP and other radical swat teams from the genital fringe have got to hit the mute button, because that caterwauling is throwing all the wrong switches out there in the vast heartland of America. Also, there's no need for members of ACT UP to throw condoms at Catholic priests. It's disrespectful, and besides, these days, most priests already have their own condoms.

And on the straight side of the ledger, right wing politicians and flaks have got to stop preaching the politics of exclusion. Pat Buchanan is so homophobic he blames global warming on the AIDS quilt.

You know something, it is time to grow up, to stop looking for bogeymen under the bed. We don't have the time to waste. I don't know if you've peeked through the Levolors lately, but we are roller-blading toward chaos with no elbow pads. The infrastructure of civilized society is unraveling faster than O.J.'s alibi. What the hell, let's try tolerance, because we need all the bright, capable people we can possibly get our hands on.

We have got to ratchet down the sexual hysteria in this country. Live and let live, folks. Let your neighbor come home, get out of his car, wave happily at you as he goes into his home, and then, you know something, forget about him or her. Let it go.

Why do we try to intellectualize sex anyway? It resides in an exalted position in the visceral pantheon because it is the Great unfigurable We don't know much about it, but we do know that the orgasm never disappoints. You've never come, and thought, "Eeeuugh, what was that?!" It's always there for you. You know that incredible feeling when you're in the midst of one of those Santino Corleone door-banging froths, one of those Arthur C. Clarke memorial fucks, where you look down at the bottom of the bed and see that big monolith, and you don't have any idea what it means, but you know something really, really important is about to happen. And the guy's got that Eddie Vedder–head shake thing going, and the woman's muttering under her breath like Donovan singing "Hurdy Gurdy Man." And you realize at that precise moment you are at the pleasurable epicenter of the Milky Way galaxy.

And then, as so frequently happens in human endeavors, one or the other sexual partners inadvertently hurts the other person by accidentally elbowing them, or leaning on their hair. The pain breaks the sexual frame of reference. We begin to decompress and intellectualize again. And when you consider sex from that narrow perspective—you see it's really such an odd, quirky little exercise. And the woman's just about to kiss her own tit, she sees you looking at her with that tilt-head look like your dog at his bowl when you change his food on him. She realizes you're no longer in the throes of it. She tries to smooth her way out, but she knows you've caught her. And she looks at you and says, "If you ever mention it, I'll kill you in your sleep, you treacherous cocksucker." And that is sex, so leave it at that and don't even try to figure it out.

Of course, that's just my opinion. I could be wrong.

schadenfreude

THE SUPREME COURT EDITED A FEDERAL LAW
against child pornography, saying there must be
proof a defendant knew the nature of the material.
Clarence Thomas did not write an opinion but did
shout out, "Will everybody stop looking at me
whenever they mention porno!"

Boy, don't you just love watching a guy like that
squirm. Isn't it funny how sometimes you hear a
story like that and it just warms your innards like a

deliciously evil hot toddy? You know what they call that? Well, the Germans have a word for it . . . "Beck's!" Actually it's called schadenfreude. And while there's no literal translation in our language, loosely stated, it means, "The malicious enjoyment of another's misfortune." Leave it to our Teutonic friends the Germans to concoct an intricate glossary of pain terminology.

Now I don't want to get off on a rant here, but what is it in people that makes them happy, somewhere under the upbringing—happy in a secret place to see hard times descend on others? And not just their enemies, but strangers, acquaintances, and even friends.

Well, truth be told, I believe we are all, oft-times, megalomaniacal green-eyed monsters who think that there is a finite amount of success floating around the universe, and who, like Miss Hathaway at the garter toss, believe that if we don't fight for position, we will perpetually be left longing for our big piece of the score pie.

Where would *People* magazine, *The Star*, and *The National Enquirer* be without schadenfreude? Don't we read these rags so we can think to ourselves, "I can't believe he got caught!" or, "Wow, my life could be a lot worse," or, "Thank you, thank you, dear God, for not making me Mickey Rourke!"

And you know it's just not common folk who dwell in it. You know who's knee-deep in schadenfreude right now?

George Bush with Clinton. You know Bush was sitting down in Houston in a condo in his undies with a big joint, watching C-SPAN. "Barbara . . . is this the North Slope, or did he just hire Gergen?! Put that purple teddy on, baby, bring ma a Corona."

Schadenfreude is as old as the Scriptures. Believe me, when the girls in the Red Sea bowling league heard that Lot's wife had morphed into a pillar of salt, the deer-lick jokes flew.

And the hottest new showplace for schadenfreude is the tabloid television shows—projectile gossiping disguised as journalism. You know, folks, "Hard Copy" is to journalism what Lieutenant William Calley was to thatched huts. Let's be honest with each other—we don't frequent these shows because we think some information exchange of consequence will occur; we watch them to reassure our-selves that there are freaks out there who are forced to eat way more shit than we do.

And when rumored troubles of the tabloid shows aren't enough, we dive into the vérité human pain shows like "Cops" and "Rescue 911" because it allows us to sit at home in a warm bed and revel in the fact that our face isn't being jammed into that wet pavement by officer Wedge Figgus of the Pensacola Police department. We will take anybody's pain. Anybody whose life's unraveling like a cheap Jamaican espadrille—just get the lens cap, baby. We need another hit.

If that seems harsh to you, one way to keep your sanity the next time you're feeling shitty about not feeling shitty about someone else feeling shitty is to remember that schadenfreude cancels itself out because others feel it just as strongly about you. There is a massive common pool of ill will out there, and we all siphon off a bit of it and smuggle it out into the common yard like dirt in the prisoner's pant legs in *The Great Escape*.

We might as well face the fact that we sometimes revel in the setbacks in other people's lives. We need to admit that that feeling has been built into the lining of the human heart from the clay model on, so that when we experience this imperfectly human joy at another's tale of woe, we won't feel freakish and broken.

It might be nasty, unkind, brutish, but schadenfreude is on the DNA map, folks, a familiar haunt on the double helix. It dwells there, because in the grand scheme, you want to know that there's a buffer between you and the tater cellar. Hey, you might not be in a first-class cabin, but let's face it, it's a good feeling to know that everyone in steerage is gonna have to wait until you get your ass in a lifeboat before they're even allowed up on deck.

Of course, that's just my opinion. I could be wrong.

parenting

I TELL YOU THERE IS NO LOVE SWEETER THAN THE love between a mother and a child. Now I know my wife loves me but I am reasonably sure that she doesn't look at me the same way she looks at them. You know it's kind of humbling because you realize at some point you're just a date that worked out.

Now I don't want to get off on a rant here, but parenting is the most important job on the planet next to keeping Gary Busey off the nation's highways.

And the reason parenting is becoming increasingly crucial is that we now live in a world that is more fucked up than Peter O'Toole on his birthday.

You know I used to scoff at the art of parenting. When I was single I was walking down the street one day in New York City and I spotted a guy with one baby in a carriage wailing like a siren, and another one master-blastered on his back in a holster; he was feeding both of them a combination of Cheerios, Zwieback crackers, and Juicy Juice from a Baggie he had Scotch-taped to his chest hair. All the while he was pullin' baby wipes out of a belly pack like a coked-up baccarat dealer going through a four-deck shoe. And I swore I would never end up like that. Well, you know something?

A couple of years later I did become a parent and guess what? I'm still not like that loser. And for that matter, I still don't have any chest hair.

But I do have a firm grasp of the fact that the most important job I'll ever do is that of parenting. It's that simple, folks. Kids are the sponge, you are the Super-soaker. You know it seems that teachers, friends, and neighbors alike know where a child's behavior is coming from. But often the parents themselves are in denial. I remember once my kid got in trouble for saying to his teacher, "What time is fucking recess?" and I remember thinking, "Now where would he fucking pick up something like that?" But so be it . . . you never did that. You're a good boy, Holden, it was a joke. Be it swearing or loving or hating, we undeniably impact our children. So I propose the following: Make parenting illegal without a license.

It would go something like this. A *man* who wanted to have a child would have to prove he was responsible, earned enough money for food and clothes for the kid, and would commit enough of his time and wisdom to assure the rest of us that the kid wouldn't end up in a Texas bell tower with a high-powered rifle and a grudge any time soon. As for the *woman*, same deal—but she has to also promise not to make him wear her dresses while she hems them, the pins sticking his tender calves, the humiliation slowly destroying his young will to be the world's funniest comedian . . . um, sorry.

And then there's the main reason, the definitive reason, the sadly serious reason that you should have to be licensed to have a child. There seems to be a shocking rise in the incidence of child abuse on this planet and I think it augers for the end of the world. I understand a man's inhumanity to man. Adults are violent amorphous blobs that careen around the planet. Occasionally they brush up against another individual and hey, their life must end. All right, I think we all dig that transaction. We are big boys and girls and we dig our own graves. But when did we start bleeding it into the innocent?

You've got to promise me if you're watching me tonight and you ever get to the point in your life where you are so puzzled, confused, and frightened that you feel the only way out is to abuse or molest a little kid, well then, you have got to kill yourself. You have got to lean into the strike zone and take one for the team.

Listen, in an age where a child can be left unsupervised in a trailer with "Beavis and Butt-head" on the TV and a book of matches within easy reach, a license to procreate starts to make some sense. If you're still unconvinced, let me put it to you another way: *Kato Kaelin is a father.*

All right? Our society is increasingly made up of people whose parents bailed out on them. You want to do something about it?

Don't bail out on your kids. How's that for a simple can-do? Rise up out of the mire of your own narcissism and get selfless, for chrissake. You want a better world?

The seeds for it are right there in your own house. Be good to those tiny humans lying there on the living room floor watching cartoons, and be good to your kids too, give them a future and they'll return the favor by giving you one in spades, my friend.

If you can stare between the stars into the blackness at heaven and say with a smile on your face, "I'll do anything and everything to be a good parent," then you're ready. Almost. Get yourself a copy of *The Lion King*. Now you're ready.

Of course, that's just my opinion. I could be wrong.

tabloids

WOW, THE TABLOIDS ARE HAVING A FIELD DAY
with O.J., aren't they? It's like manna from
Brentwood.

Now I don't want to get off on a rant here, but
we've all been trapped fifty people deep in the
"nine items or less" line at the Alpha Beta and just
when you think you've spotted the Northwest Passage, i.e., the cash register, the troglodyte ahead of

you begins rifling through a grease-stained doughnut bag and produces a curled-up, coffee-soiled check from the Bank of Communicable Diseases.

The woman behind the cash register initiates an ID check that would make the Rio Grande border patrol seem like greeters at Caesars Palace.

You're now stuck in a quagmire that even Robert McNamara could have spotted, and you hate yourself for getting tangled in this gill net of inefficiency.

Just then, when all appears to be lost, it catches your eye, grail-like in its majesty, the journalistic golden fleece, the tabloid rack. Your eyes pass over the appetizing array of completely unbelievable headlines. JIMMY CAAN SHAVES BACK WITH GARDEN WEASEL, CLAUDIA SCHIFFER TO MARRY CARROT TOP, SONNY BONO ELECTED TO CONGRESS.

As you begin to leaf through this collection of unholy writ you think to yourself, "God, who reads this shit?" Then the bolt of realization strikes you like a Joan Crawford coat hanger—*You* read this shit! There's just something about the tabloids that appeals to your Mr. Hyde, your flip side, your lower cortex monkey brain. Now, granted, we all have a fantasy that we're too busy catching up on our back issues of *Deconstructionist Philosophy Monthly* to get down and dish the demented dirt, but we all read the tabloids. It's a guilty pleasure that's right up there with digging the hooks in Abba songs.

Where else but in the tabloids would you find such sage advice as the horoscope that reads "Leo—stay indoors, don't breathe." Or such wonderful diets as the "Eat Shit and *Live* System!" Where else would you see a full-page photo of Danielle Brisebois' head on William Devane's body. You know, being a tabloid photographer has got to be the lowest possible rung on the photojournalistic ladder. I mean think about it. On the one hand there are Stieglitzian masters out there doing brilliant photo essays on the insurgency in Chad, the plight of the migrant worker, the tragedy that is Rwanda.

You're sitting there at your dining room table doing still lifes of a yam shaped like Hitler. What concentric circle of Scavullo hell does that get you into?

Do you know the *Enquirer* actually has subscribers?

Clue me in on what sort of specific genetic anomaly it is who feels the need to subscribe to the fucking *Enquirer.* These are the same people who tape QVC.

And then there are the really mega-freaky publications like *Weekly World News* that are so deranged parakeets will actually hold their shit in until something else is placed in the bottom of their cage.

You know, these tabloids even have classified ads. I saw one once that actually said, "Learn how to avoid rip-offs . . . send five dollars." Now you gotta be a real piece of Samsonite to answer this ad. "Hey, honey. I'll send ten, we'll be doubly protected." Look, I'll be the first one to tell you that the tabloids are to journalism what the Clapper is to electronics. But when was the last time you saw your precious little *New York Times* run a front-page photo of a vampire. Huh? Never.

From every scope of the intellectual spectrum, from nuclear physicists all the way down to stupid nuclear physicists, everyone cherishes the tabloids. So don't try to get me into some pipe-smoking, Jeff Greenfield–mediated panel discussion on "the tabloids erosion of our sacred journalistic traditions." Tabloids aren't journalism. And if journalism schools keep kicking out reporters who've substituted attitude and ego in place of a reporter's notebook, *newspapers* aren't gonna be journalism real soon either.

The tabloids are pure marzipan; they're entertaining, but only if you remember to follow just one shampoo—simple instruction—*don't believe a fucking word you read in them.* Any of 'em. If you react to the tabloids with anything but peals of laughter, if you actually take these oil-pan blotters seriously, you need to reattach yourself to the planet, my friend, because you are two months out from your pledge week with the Michigan Militia, okay? Oh, and by the way, if you ever come across the story about Dennis Miller's sexual obsession with Doberman pinschers, just remember, all I said was, "I like dogs."

Of course that's just my opinion. I could be wrong.